Concord's Great Meadows

A Human History

Carol E. Gupta

This work is dedicated to
Gautam and Maya.

Contact the author at HayMeadows Press, P.O. Box 485, Concord, MA 01742 or at HayMeadowsPress@aol.com

Book design: Christine Reynolds/Reynolds Design, Waltham, MA
Cover photography credits: Jack Garrison: photograph courtesy of Concord Museum, Concord, MA. www.concordmuseum.org; Samuel Hoar: photograph courtesy of the Social Circle in Concord; Ed Moses: photograph courtesy of Ed Moses

First Printing May 2004

Additional copies of this book are available by mail. Send $14.50 each (which includes tax and postage) to Carol Gupta, HayMeadows Press, P.O. Box 485, Concord, MA 01742

Printed in Victoria, Canada.

Note for Librarians: a cataloguing record for this book that includes Dewey Classification and US Library of Congress numbers is available from the National Library of Canada. The complete cataloguing record can be obtained from the National Library's online database at: www.nlc-bnc.ca/amicus/index-e.html

ISBN: 1-4120-2335-1

TRAFFORD

This book was published *on-demand* in cooperation with Trafford Publishing. On-demand publishing is a unique process and service of making a book available for retail sale to the public taking advantage of on-demand manufacturing and Internet marketing. **On-demand publishing** includes promotions, retail sales, manufacturing, order fulfilment, accounting and collecting royalties on behalf of the author.

Suite 6E, 2333 Government St., Victoria, B.C. V8T 4P4, CANADA

Phone	250-383-6864	Toll-free	1-888-232-4444 (Canada & US)
Fax	250-383-6804	E-mail	sales@trafford.com
Web site www.trafford.com		TRAFFORD PUBLISHING IS A DIVISION OF TRAFFORD HOLDINGS, LTD.	
Trafford Catalogue # 04-0163		www.trafford.com/robots/04-0163.html	

10   9   8   7   6   5   4   3   2

Acknowlegements

I was prompted to write this chronicle by a simple curiosity about the people who had preceded me in the Great Meadows. Being neither historian nor archaeologist, I had no idea how easy it is to blunder when one is trying to reconstruct the past. Scholars Shirley Blancke, Tom Blanding, Dena Dincauze, Brian Donahue, and Leslie Perrin Wilson rescued me from confusion and error and introduced me to new avenues of exploration.

Charlie Dee not only allowed me to handle his exquisite collection of artifacts, he showed me the area where he had found them. Brownie Borden dug into family archives for books, photographs, and documents that would acquaint me with Dick Borden and his legacy, and Betsy Borden Carlson contributed written recollections. Though in the last stage of the illness that claimed her, Virginia Hoar Frecha made the effort to visit me and talk about her childhood in the Great Meadows. And Ed Moses, with characteristic courtesy, gave me all the time I needed to understand the role of the refuge manager and his particular part in the Great Meadows story.

Maya Gupta rendered invaluable assistance in creating several of the Great Meadows maps. Constance Putnam edited my subultimate, penultimate, and final manuscripts, and suggested changes that added to the coherence and clarity of the finished work.

So many others contributed to this project. I hesitate to begin naming them for fear of leaving someone out — an easy thing to do given that virtually everyone I asked for help gave it unstintingly.

Thank you all.

Contents

List of Maps

List of Photographs

Introduction

A Walk on the Dike

The mudflats of Concord's Great Meadows abound, on this early September day, with some of the largest and most elegant of the freshwater birds. Great blue herons — named for their four-foot height and blue-gray plumage — wait among the cattails, their stillness a perfect camouflage. Suddenly, one of the herons snaps up a frog and, with a huge gulp, swallows it. Several great and snowy egrets, cousins of the great blues, also stalk frogs and small fish. Now and then, the egrets rise up in a dazzle of white wings.

Feeding among the great blues and, at first glance, indistinguishable from them, is a surprise visitor. The red patch on the visitor's face and crown, and a bustle of gray plumage over its rump, identify it as a sandhill crane — a *lost* sandhill crane, apparently, because this species migrates through the plains states to reach its winter home along the Gulf coast. Birding enthusiasts line the dike, their spotting scopes and binoculars trained on this rarity.

More typical Great Meadows birds — Canada geese, mallards and teals, wood ducks, killdeer — feed in the shallows. An elusive marsh wren rattles from its hiding place in the cattails. Red-winged blackbirds flit busily between trees and cattails, whistling *tee-err, tee-err* or crooning *o-ka-leee* when they alight. Gliding above it all, a marsh hawk looks for its next meal.

At the end of the main dike and around the corner, another surprise awaits the walker. Scores of northern leopard frogs doze on the grassy path. Their disguise of green-varying-to-brown skin and dark "leopard" spots makes them almost invisible. The minute they sense a footfall, they leap in unpredictable directions, and the path comes alive in a frenzy of frogs. A jogger finds herself trapped in the midst of them, and she slows to avoid stepping on a frog. When one of them vaults onto her bare leg, she squeals and hurries on.

The Great Meadows in Concord is a wetland ecosystem consisting of approximately 250 acres operated by the U.S. Department of the Interior's Fish and Wildlife Service and 70 adjacent acres of privately owned land, where I am fortunate enough to make my home. These wetlands are more than just a precious resource to Concord; they are the nucleus of the 3,863.45-acre (as of January 9, 2004) Great Meadows National Wildlife Refuge (GMNWR) that extends into seven other towns: Bedford, Billerica, Carlisle, Framingham, Lincoln, Sudbury, and Wayland.

Overview

Most visitors to the Great Meadows come to observe and enjoy its birds and other animal life. Since human beings have always been drawn to animals — as a source of food, as objects of sport or aesthetic delight, or as subjects of scientific inquiry — it is not surprising that the history of the Great Meadows is very much a human story.

This chronicle begins with the first people to arrive in the Great Meadows 13,000 to 11,000 years ago. In that resource-scarce, postglacial world, the Great Meadows was but one stopping place in early people's search for food. Beginning about 11,000 years ago, the climate started to become more temperate, and plants and animals became more plentiful, enabling people to settle in for longer stays. About 3,000 years ago, humans began to stay long enough to raise crops. In every era, prehistoric people left behind some of the material they used in their daily lives, and these artifacts, as interpreted by archaeologists, provide a glimpse into the lives of the first people to pass through the Great Meadows.

From the 17th century onward, history would be measured in centuries rather than millennia, and would be recorded in words. The arrival of the Europeans (and their diseases) in the New World brought about the eventual demise of the indigenous peoples and their culture. The English farmers who established Concord Plantation in 1635, supplanting the native Algonquians, turned to the river meadows as a source of hay for their livestock. From the beginning, Great Meadows hay was an integral component of Concord's agricultural economy, and it remained so for more than 200 years.

In 1761, John Jack became the first of several ex-slaves to move to the ridge overlooking the Great Meadows. Caesar and Rose Robbins came next, and Jack Garrison and his family joined them. When Caesar and Rose died, Peter Hutchinson and his family moved into the Robbinses' home. These Great Meadows African Americans were part of a small community of black people who lived in Concord during the late 18th and 19th centuries.

By the first half of the 19th century, people began coming to the Great Meadows — not for food, fodder, or a place to live — but to enjoy its natural beauty and the marvels of its wildlife. Naturalist Henry David Thoreau recorded his observations of the Great Meadows and its denizens in his journals. Henry's friend, philosopher Ralph Waldo Emerson, explored the Great Meadows with his brothers, and later memorialized them in his poetry. In the latter half of the 19th century, the pioneering ornithologist William Brewster from the Harvard Museum of Comparative Zoology used the Great Meadows as his field laboratory.

In 1927, Sam Hoar arrived in the Great Meadows with a new idea: he would transform these marshy lowlands into a series of ponds that would attract migratory waterfowl for hunting and bird watching. Sam Hoar acquired the Great Meadows, piece by piece, until he owned all the land he needed to create his wetlands habitat. In 1944, he donated almost 80% of it to the Department of the Interior, U.S. Fish and Wildlife Service, for use as a wildlife sanctuary. From that point on, the Great Meadows would be divided into the "public" and the "private" sides. Dick Borden, a wildlife cinematographer and conservationist, followed Sam Hoar in the private Great Meadows. Ed Moses became the first resident manager of the Great Meadows National Wildlife Refuge. His successors included Arthur Tibbs, Larry Malone, Grady Hocutt, Linda Gintoli, David Beall, Lloyd Culp, and . . . Ed Moses, who returned to the Great Meadows for a second term to finish out his career with the U.S. Fish and Wildlife Service.

PART I

The Old Ones and
What They Left Behind

Two Canada geese are fighting a high-stakes duel in a secluded corner of Concord's Great Meadows. Twenty or more geese have formed a ring around them, murmuring uneasily. The combatants themselves are silent as they circle each other in a deadly pas de deux. First one strikes the neck of the other with open beak; then his opponent strikes back. Round they go — jab, counter-jab, dodge, another jab — on and on with mounting ferocity. The conflict gives every appearance of a fight-to-the-death.

A woman stops abruptly in her daily walk to witness this unprecedented sight. "What can be going on?" she wonders. She is well acquainted with the noisy territorial squabbles of geese. She has seen the way the male bends his neck in a mild warning, pumps his head in a more aggressive gesture, and even charges other males when seriously threatened. But never has she seen such a ritualized battle, or one fought with such apparently lethal intent. She thinks, "More is at issue here than a few square yards of pond — something deeper, older."

Initially, the antagonists were evenly matched, but now one has gained the advantage, striking twice to his opponent's once. The weakening goose takes blow after blow, but fights on. The woman thinks fleetingly that she should intervene to save the weaker goose, but something holds her back. She tells herself, "I am an outsider. I have no place in this," and, shuddering slightly, returns to her walk.

The next morning, life on the pond is back to normal. The woman watches the female geese pluck grasses for their nests, while the males patrol their territory with only an occasional display of machismo. It is a beguilingly domestic scene; the geese give no hint of their darker side. The woman reflects that she will never know how the duel ended, or why it happened.

There is so much that we, too, will never know. The birds and animals that currently frequent the Great Meadows, even the ubiquitous Canada geese, remain only partially knowable to us. How much more difficult it is, then, to decipher the lives of the people who preceded us in the Great Meadows by thousands of years, especially since they left behind no written record of their activities. Happily for this history, they did leave us some of the tools they used in their everyday lives. In fact, the Great Meadows area has yielded the richest concentration of artifacts of any Concord site. This physical evidence, considered in the light of the traditions and oral history of living Native Americans, enables archaeologists to form a picture of human life in the prehistoric era.

The Pioneers of the Pleistocene

Men and women first arrived in the Great Meadows 13,000 to 11,000 years ago, after the mantle of ice that had covered New England for 60,000 years finally receded. The melting glacier deposited soil, the birds and wind brought seeds, and eventually shrubs and other herbaceous plants took root. Over time, the animals began to arrive, each kind in search of the plants or creatures below it in the food chain. And so it was that one day a new animal, *Homo sapiens,* appeared on the landscape, also in quest of food.

As Dena F. Dincauze points out in *From Musketaquid to Concord,* the very fact that these pioneers (known as Paleoindians to archaeologists) reached the Northeast was itself remarkable. Traveling without benefit of compass, map, or technical gear, the Paleoindians crossed the continent from the south or the west. They forded rushing rivers, circumvented glacial lakes and wetlands, and threaded their way through forbidding, ice-clad mountains. We cannot know what inspired their migration, what they strove to escape or achieve, but we can be sure that getting here at all required courage and ingenuity. Once they arrived, further challenges awaited them. The glacier had wrought a new world never before inhabited by humans. These earliest people had to invent a way of life that would sustain them in this untried environment.

Probably no more than a few hundred people lived in the Northeast during the period called the Pleistocene (13,000 to 11,000 years ago) by archaeologists. Most lived on the continental shelf exposed because the north polar ice-cap had absorbed much of the planet's water. The marshes and estuaries of the continental shelf yielded a bountiful food supply. Nonetheless, the Paleoindians would regularly make inland forays to hunt caribou and other large mammals.

We know that Paleoindians came to the Great Meadows and camped on the ridge running along its south and eastern edge (see map) because they left behind fluted spear points characteristic of the Pleistocene era. According to Esther K. Braun and David P. Braun writing in *The First Peoples of the Northeast,* this type of leaf-shaped spear point with a flaked groove running up the middle "is so distinctive that any time an archaeologist finds one someplace, he or she knows that a Paleoindian passed by there long ago."

The steep drop from the ridge to the low-lying marshland of the Great Meadows is a good example of what geologists call "the ice contact face," the place where the glacier stopped. (See map) The high ground overlooking the marshes may have appealed to

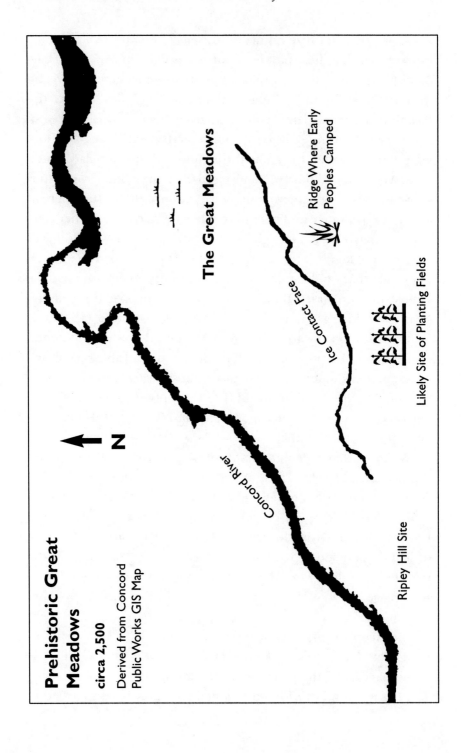

Prehistoric Great Meadows

circa 2,500

Derived from Concord Public Works GIS Map

N

Concord River

The Great Meadows

Ice Contact Face

Ridge Where Early Peoples Camped

Likely Site of Planting Fields

Ripley Hill Site

the Paleoindians as a campsite because it offered a dry stopping place in a wet terrain. The site had the added advantage of lying at the intersection of two ecological niches — the plains that extended from the ridge and the marshlands below it — and being within easy reach of a third, the river. Three such niches could mean triple the food-gathering potential. Even so, the Great Meadows in the Pleistocene was hardly a land of plenty. Its flora included ground covers such as groundnuts and other tuberous root plants, and, on the upland, berry-producing shrubs and pine trees. It was home to waterfowl and small mammals, such as rabbits. Occasionally, larger game, such as elk, caribou, and moose, browsed on the plains behind the ridge.

If we could visit this campsite on a fall day 11,000 years ago, we might find a hunting party consisting of two or three families. The people appear fully modern to our eye, but they are far more skillful than we would be in extracting the maximum sustenance out of a spare environment. As the women forage in the lowlands, they hear their men shouting on the ridge, and from this they know that the men are in pursuit of an animal. The women stand up and crane their necks to watch the hunters drive a caribou over the edge of the bluff. The quarry stumbles and is down; the hunters quickly finish the kill, using spears with hard stone points. These Paleoindian men are successful hunters because they know their prey intimately — what it eats and the habitat it frequents, how it moves through its territory, and its behavior under attack.

Once the caribou is slain, each member of the band gets to work converting various parts of the animal into the necessities of life. The men carve the meat and create tools from its bones. The women scrape the skin and fashion it into apparel and containers for storage and cooking; several skins together might be used in making a shelter. The pioneers pause here, on the edge of the Great Meadows, only so long as they can extract foodstuffs and other materials from the land. When they move on, they will probably follow a route they have taken many times before.

The Paleoindian culture lasted for roughly two millennia. But gradually the environment changed, and the people changed with it. A warming climate made it possible for southern vegetation to move into the Northeast, species by species. The conifers — spruce, then pine and hemlock — arrived in the early Pleistocene. As the climate warmed still more, oaks and other broad-leafed trees found their way into the region, and with them, the animal and plant life that would thrive in such a habitat. These changes gave rise to a new culture — the settlers — who succeeded the hunter-gatherers of the Pleistocene. This next epoch of New England history, the Archaic era, spanned the period from 11,000 years ago to 3,000 years ago.

The Settlers of the Archaic Era

A revisit to the Great Meadows campsite near the end of the Archaic period, about 4,000 years ago, reveals a far greener landscape than existed in the Pleistocene. A rich mix of tubers, shrubs, rushes, sedges, and grasses covers much of the marshland, and deciduous trees grow near the river and on the ridge. Several families are camped here, and the greater variety of natural resources will enable them to settle in for much longer than their Paleoindian forebears. The population of the Concord area has reached an all-time high, not only because of the greater assortment of foodstuffs, but also because the coastal population has probably been forced inland by the rising sea level and the corresponding narrowing of the continental shelf.

As the people go about their daily tasks, they use tools they have designed to make the most of the new materials and edibles. The men and boys forage in the river, using pronged spears and weighted nets to catch fish, frogs, turtles, and water snakes. Nearby, a father and son gouge out a log to make a canoe: the river provides not only food but also a corridor for transportation and communication. Back at the camp, women pound nuts and seeds with mortar and pestle, and they use knives and scrapers to gut and scale fish and to scrape hair and fat from deerskin. This concentrated use of the Great Meadows and other Concord sites during the Archaic era is borne out by the number of artifacts from that period discovered by antiquarians.

The Farmers of the Woodland Era

Eventually, the farming practices developed in Peru and Mexico spread across the North American continent, and the inhabitants of the Northeast began to cultivate crops. At first, the native people grew squash, gourds (for use as vessels), and sunflowers. Much later, in what is known as the Woodland period (3,000 years ago to the time of contact with Europeans), they began to grow maize and beans. As the farmers became attached to particular fields with especially productive soils, they settled into villages for the entire growing season. Cultivated crops provided a stable source of food that could last the winter. The Woodland people also relied on wild foods to round out their diet and were, as a result, much healthier than native peoples of, for example, the Southwest, who ate only cultivated foods. These early farmers also began making pots, at first from soapstone and later from the more readily available clay.

The people of the Woodland period left only a few traces on the ridge where their ancestors had camped, although that ridge is the likely location of their planting fields. Edward Emerson (writing in the *Memoirs of the Social Circle in Concord, Second Series*) remarks, "Above these [Great] meadows and behind the hill on low bluffs were old Indian cornfields grown up to oak and birch wood. . ." Those cornfields were probably located at the western edge of what the English colonists called the "Great Field."

A small plateau on the north side of Ripley Hill in the far southwestern corner of the Great Meadows yielded more plentiful evidence of the Woodland people's lives. In 1926, workers excavating for Sam Hoar's house (see Part V) uncovered two parallel rows of fire pits paved with pebbles. From each of these pits, trenches extended which ended in large unpaved hollows. Several other fire or storage depressions were exposed, one of which was more than five feet deep and eight feet in diameter. In addition to the pits, the workmen also found four graves. The first two of these contained the bodies of women, one about 30 and the other about 15 years of age. The remains were boxed and sent to the Peabody Museum at Harvard for study; later, they were reportedly conveyed to the Concord Public Library, but their whereabouts have been unknown for more than 30 years. Unfortunately, Massachusetts did not, at that time, have statutes protecting Indian burial sites. The other two graves were left undisturbed.

The Ripley Hill settlement was no temporary encampment, like the Paleoindian and Archaic sites mentioned above, but "the site of intense Indian activity," as archaeologist Benjamin L. Smith noted. The burials support the notion of permanence and territoriality. Additionally, the existence of more than 12 pits laid out in such an orderly way argues for a larger, more permanent, and more complex community than we have seen previously. Such a sizeable facility for processing and storing food would have been needed if crops — probably corn, maize, and beans — were grown nearby, most likely in the fields mentioned by Edward Emerson. This Woodland era site represents the end of the pre-European period in the Great Meadows.

The domestic debris left behind at Ripley Hill yielded hundreds of artifacts that were carried away by collectors. Many are lost to us today. Of those remaining, a soapstone face effigy pendant of a type rare in Massachusetts stands out. This pendant (pictured right), used perhaps in ceremonies of healing or mourning, is the only representation of a human face we have from the first 13,000 years of human history in the Great Meadows.

Face effigy pendant: Late Woodland; Ripley Hill, Concord. Soapstone. Photo courtesy of Concord Museum, Concord, MA. www.concordmuseum.org

The Antiquarians

As noted earlier, we are able to evoke this picture of pre-European activity in the Great Meadows largely on the basis of the physical materials early people left behind: spear points, scrapers, knives, gouges, plummets (weights), mortars and pestles, clay pots. Most of the surviving Indian relics from the Great Meadows can be found in the late Benjamin L. Smith's collection owned by the Concord Museum and in the private collection of amateur antiquarian Charlie Dee.

Charlie, who is 80 years old, started digging for "arrowheads" (the collector's generic term for arrowheads, spear points, and similar artifacts) as a result of a school assignment when he was in fifth grade. He has never really stopped. His current collection contains more than 300 pieces. It spans a 13,000-year period and represents the Paleoindian, Archaic, and Woodland eras. Most of his artifacts came from a one- or two-mile stretch, once owned by his grandfather, on the very ridge where the Paleoindian hunters and Archaic settlers camped and the Woodland farmers tilled their maize fields.

The oldest and possibly most valuable pieces in Charlie's collection are three fluted spear points from the Pleistocene era.

Turning over plummets and gouges, grinding stones, and celts (axes), Charlie remarks, "I've gotten a thrill out of every arrowhead I've ever collected." To hold one of Charlie Dee's artifacts is to feel a physical link with the human being who used it five, ten, or even twelve thousand years ago. It *is* a thrill.

On the Brink – The Algonquians of Musketaquid

On the eve of European arrival, life in the Great Meadows goes on much as it has for thousands of years. The natives — Algonquian-speaking people organized under Sagamore Tahattawan — hunt, fish, and forage using the accumulated knowledge of their predecessors.

On a spring day in the year 1600, the men are at the river, fishing with plummet-weighted nets and forked spears for alewife, eels, turtles, and various year-round fish. Some of the women are at work in the marshes, digging out cattail shoots, an asparagus-like vegetable. By mid-summer, the meadows will yield other nutritious foods, such as the tubers of the arrowhead plant (also known as "duck-potato"), which the women will boil in a clay pot to make a potato-like dish. Some of them may even gather water parsnip — but carefully, because of its similarity to the poisonous water hemlock — for use as a cooked vegetable.

In the fall, cranberries and wild rice ripen in the meadows. The women will gather rushes, cattails, and coarse grasses for use in making baskets and bags, as well as mats to cover house frames. Fall will also bring migratory waterfowl, which the men will catch with nets or hunt with bow and arrow, a relatively recent addition to their weaponry. Thus, Tahattawan and his people are able to extract resources from the Great Meadows at least three seasons of the year. They will supplement these foodstuffs with corn, beans, and squash cultivated by the women in upland fields on the ridge overlooking the meadows.

The Algonquian civilization appears to have been self-sustaining and within the land's capacity to support. Given a relatively stable population, it might have endured for many more centuries, had it not been for the advent of a new group of pioneers — the Europeans. European diseases felled as many as 90% of the local inhabitants even before the arrival of English settlers in Musketaquid — "the place where the river flows through the grasses." The Algonquians' traditional way of life was all but extinguished in less than 50 years from the founding of Concord. They left Musketaquid; today, some of their descendants may be found among the Nipmucks of Central Massachusetts.

*The **Author**, holding a pestle used for pounding and grinding grain, and amateur antiquarian **Charlie Dee**, holding a deep-groove ax head and a gouge. (Photo by Susan Dee)*

PART II

The New Pioneers

The river is waking. The first rays of the sun begin to burn off the night vapors and a dozen voices sing their morning songs. Tree swallows call *cheet, chi-veet* as they wheel over the water, their back feathers gleaming with the colors of sky and tree and earth. The air still rings with the silvery carillon of spring peepers, who have sung the night away and are now welcoming in the new spring day. And amid the grasses along the riverbank, two muskrats make little whimpering noises as they swim and dive.

The sound of a paddle scraping against wood intrudes upon the matinal chorus, and a canoe emerges from the thinning mist. Captain Simon Willard is scouting for a congenial site on which to build a new settlement. So far, he has liked what he's seen of the place the Algonquians call Musketaquid: plenty of alewife running in three rivers, an abundance of beavers, several mill-worthy streams, and miles and miles of river meadows. This one, for example — a pale green carpet stretching a mile or more along the river — this one will winter a big herd, Willard thinks as he scrutinizes the Great Meadow*. He is perhaps the first Englishman to set eyes on it. His further explorations reveal Indian planting fields on the uplands and extensive woodlands throughout. Here in Musketaquid, Willard muses, is everything needed to establish the Massachusetts Bay Colony's first inland plantation.

---

*In colonial times, the area we know as "the Great Meadows" was referred to in the singular — "the Great Meadow."

The Planters

Simon Willard, though only 30 years old, was an exemplary leader for such an enterprise. As a fur trader and soldier, a man thoroughly at home in the wilderness and on good terms with the Indians, he was uniquely equipped to help others adapt to the New World. He joined forces with the Reverend Peter Bulkeley, for every plantation in the Colony required a spiritual leader. The 52 year-old Bulkeley proved to be a worthy partner in the founding venture. He had been forced to leave an affluent and comfortable life in Bedfordshire because he insisted on practicing Puritanism in defiance of the Anglican Church. In the New World, he generously invested in Concord Plantation, endured unaccustomed physical hardship, and remained in the infant community even after Puritanism prevailed in England and he could have returned to his former life.

Willard and Bulkeley recruited another 10 to 12 men and their families, emigrants from various corners of England — Northumberland, Yorkshire, Kingston-on-Thames, Derbyshire, Kent, Surrey, and Sussex. A few of the men, like Thomas Flint, were wealthy, but most were yeoman farmers who had come to the New World hungry for land and eager to escape the predations of the Church of England. The Concord founders were all part of the great migration of Puritans from England to the New World that took place in the early to mid-17th century.

The Great and General Court that governed the Bay Colony gave these pioneers permission to establish Concord on September 2,* 1635, with the following order:

> that there shall be a plantation at Musketaquid and that
> there shall be 6 miles of land square to belong to it . . .
> and the name of the place is changed and hereafter to
> be called Concord.

---

* The discrepancy between Concord's official "birthday," September 12th, and the date of the court order can be explained by England's conversion from the Julian to the Gregorian Calendar in 1754.

The actual date of the settlers' arrival in Concord has not been established, but their presence in Musketaquid in September of 1636 is a matter of record. The immigrants ceremoniously purchased their land from the Algonquians in May of 1637 for a packet of "wampumpeage" — hatchets, knives, and various items of English-style clothing. Depositions sworn in Court by both Englishmen and Indians and entered into the records of Middlesex County a half century later attest to this transaction.

As soon as the new arrivals addressed their basic survival needs, they set about surveying and dividing their six square miles. This process of apportionment — the First Division* — continued as new families immigrated to Concord. Each one of the Concord families received a houselot, planting fields, and several meadow lots.

Meadow and field were the essential components of the agricultural order, with cattle the link between them. The cycle started with meadow hay, which nourished the livestock through the winter months, when pastures were bare. At the same time, the cattle provided vital sustenance in the form of milk, cheese, and meat for the yeoman families during those same lean months. In the spring, oxen pulled the plow to ready the soil for planting. Then manure was applied to the planting fields to fertilize the crops. Manure was especially crucial because the soils of Concord's upland planting fields proved to be nutrient-poor. Without hay, the cattle could not thrive and there would be insufficient manure. Without adequate manure, there would be a poor harvest.

This relationship between hay, cattle, and crops was an agricultural verity into the 19th century. Interestingly, the land-use

---

* The original papers documenting the First Division have been lost. Charles Walcott (see Sources) was one of the first to try to piece together this information; Brian Donahue is probably the most recent.

patterns engendered by it were very different in colonial Concord than in, say, the American Midwest. Concord's first proprietors adopted an English commons system of farming. In his forthcoming book, *The Great Meadow: Farmers and the Land in Colonial Concord, Massachusetts,* Brian Donahue describes how the English model was realized in the First Division:

> A birds-eye view of landholdings in Concord about 1650 is a bit startling. Something very much resembling a classical English common field village, in all its intricate complexity, had been set down in the midst of the American forest. Some fifty long, narrow houselots formed a tight nucleus within a mile of the meeting house. . . Beyond the houselots lay the upland tillage lots of the town, mostly collected into one great and several lesser general fields, with only a few detached lots about the outskirts. Nearly two hundred mowing lots flanked the watercourses throughout the town, clustering along Elm Brook, Mill Brook, Spencer's Brook, and of course, the rivers — culminating in the Great Meadow. Surrounding everything else, covering three-quarters of the land in the infant community were the commons, composed of upland hardwood forest, pitch pine plains, and spruce and cedar swamps.

This picture is strikingly different from the one produced by land usage patterns in the American Midwest, where nucleated farms were the rule from the beginning. In colonial Concord, the houses clustered together in the village center, while the fields and meadows were scattered, seemingly at random, over the width and breadth of Concord. More remarkable still is that 75 percent of the total land grant was dedicated to common pasturage and woodland.

The Great Meadow

As the largest river meadow, the Great Meadow was one of colonial Concord's chief assets. Its proximity to the town center made it especially valuable. Some of the first proprietors of land in the Great Meadow were Nathaniel Ball; Humphrey Barrett; William Buss; William Buttrick; John Hartwell; John Heywood; Robert Meriam; and John, Joshua, and Timothy Wheeler. The reader will recognize that many of these early Concordians have been memorialized in Concord street names and places — Ball's Hill, Barrett's Mill Road, Hartwell Tavern, Heywood Street and Meadow, Meriam's Corner, Timothy Wheeler House, etc.

In the First Division (see map), the Great Meadow was parceled into more than 20 narrow strips, each of which extended from the Concord River (or the "Great River" as it was then called) to the edge of the ridge where the Great Field was located. The meadow lots, like the planting fields, were separately tended and harvested by their owners, but managed jointly. It is likely that some of the mowing strips were fenced, or partially fenced, to secure a space for cattle to graze. After the hay had been reaped in late summer and early fall, the farmers would put their cattle to graze on the aftermath.

Since the mowing lots were laid out elbow-to-elbow, farmers often had to drive their cattle across a neighbor's property to get to their own lot. Cattle worry little about whose grass they are munching, and their passage through the neighbor's lot often resulted in damage to the hay and ill will between the property holders. The matter was resolved by requiring each proprietor to build a private way into his property from the upland (Great Field) side of the Great Meadow. Another source of friction was the occasional necessity of pulling a cart through a neighbor's mowing strip while his cattle were grazing. The risk was that the cattle might escape while the gate was open. To solve that

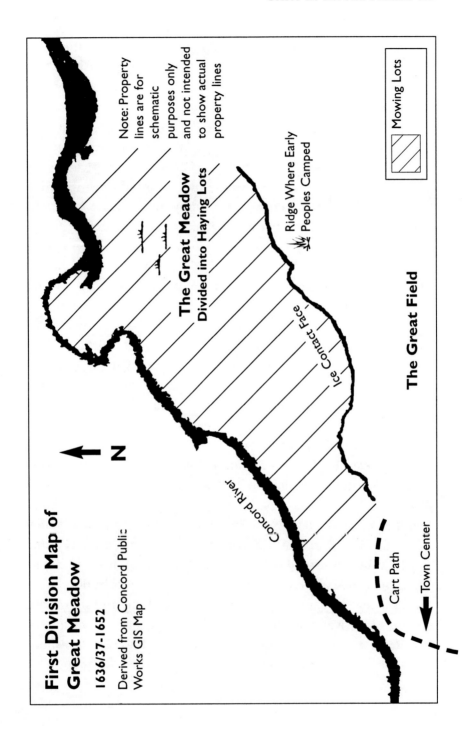

First Division Map of Great Meadow

1636/37-1652

Derived from Concord Public Works GIS Map

N

Note: Property lines are for schematic purposes only and not intended to show actual property lines

The Great Meadow Divided into Haying Lots

Ridge Where Early Peoples Camped

Ice Contact Face

Concord River

The Great Field

Cart Path

Town Center

Mowing Lots

problem, the proprietors agreed to build a cart path on the river-bank. These instances of cooperative problem identification and resolution were codified in a 1669 written agreement between the proprietors of the Great Meadow.

A proprietor of land in the Great Meadow would own three to five mowing lots in other parts of town. William Buss, for example, held 14 acres in the Great Meadow, 3 acres in South Meadow, 12 in Nut Meadow, 21 in Fairhaven, and 3 in another unspecified location. Why this dispersion of meadow parcels? We can posit that different meadows became harvest-ready at different times. Scattered meadows would enable the mowers to extend their reaping season over a longer period. Also, if the hay crop failed in one meadow, the farmer would have the backup of his other meadow acreages.

Buss's total meadow holding — 53 acres — was typical for Concord's husbandmen, yet no farmer, regardless of his endowment of sons, could have mowed so much hay by hand. Probably a good part of each meadow was unmowable. Plant species that were inferior from a bovine perspective dominated large sections of the mowing lots, and a farmer needed 30 to 50 meadow acres to yield a sufficiency of fodder.

The Great Meadow, no doubt, had its share of scrubby or otherwise undesirable vegetation, but its grasses were of high quality. The Great Meadow was not, however, exempt from another problem that plagued all of Concord's mowing fields: wetness. When the farmers tried to mow the river meadows, they discovered that much of the grass stood in water and was inaccessible or unusable. The Concord River has, throughout most of its history, flooded its meadows every year or two. Spring rains and melting snow wash soil into the river, and the river in turn inundates the meadows, providing a valuable infusion of nutrients. However, the waters must recede quickly for the growing season to be long enough for a good yield of hay.

And that is precisely what does not happen. The Concord River is a slow-moving stream, dropping only one or two feet in its 15-mile voyage to the Merrimack River. Moreover, six miles downstream from Concord, it meets the Fordway Bar, a bedrock ledge that further impedes the river's flow. For these reasons, the river does not evacuate floodwaters quickly, and the meadow grasses remained submerged far into the summer.

It did not take the farmers long to identify the Fordway Bar (which they called "the Falls" because of the waterfall created by the ledge) as a scourge upon their meadows. As early as 1636, they petitioned the General Court for assistance in cutting through the ledge. The Court ruled, somewhat inexplicably, that the expenses for deepening the river channel at the Falls should, in part, be borne by farmers and town dwellers *above* Concord.

Apparently, no further action was taken until a second petition in 1644, filed in tandem with the recently incorporated town of Sudbury, when the Court appointed joint sewer commissioners. Their charge was. . .

> to set some order which may conduce to the better
> surveying, improving,and draining of the meadows,
> and saving and preserving of the hay there gotten,
> either by draining the same, or otherwise, and to pro-
> portion the charges layed out about it as equally and
> justly (only upon them that own land) as they in their
> wisdom shall see meete.

The farmers never conquered the Fordway Bar. However, under the direction of successive generations of sewer commissioners, they did manage "to set some order" to the meadows. By such means as ditching their mowing lots, dredging sandbars in the river, and cutting weeds on the riverbank, the farmers eventually improved the drainage in their meadows and thereby increased their hay yields.

A Second Division of Land

Concord's first 20 years were trying ones for the founders — at times desperately so. The New England winters were longer and harsher, the summers hotter and dryer, the meadows wetter, and the tilling fields poorer than in England or than they ever could have imagined. Many of their number, including several children, did not survive the first hard winters. A further sorrow was the exodus, in 1644, of about one seventh of Concord's population to Fairfield, Connecticut, under the leadership of the Reverend John Jones.

In time, the pioneers adapted to New England conditions and began to make a living off their land. The little village began to grow, and pressure from this growth brought about a Second Division, in which the commons were to be parceled out to individual property owners. For the purposes of this division, the town was carved into three "quarters," with the Great Meadow being in the East Quarter. Landowners from each of the quarters were to agree on land assignments by majority rule. The principles governing the Second Division were: 1) Householders would receive three acres of the commons for every acre of First Division land they owned; 2) Each husbandman would receive upland adjacent to his meadow; and 3) Access to meadow properties would be preserved; established cartways were to be honored.

According to Brian Donahue, the landholders had two objectives for this Second Division: "The first was to secure greater individual control over particularly valuable resources, such as white oak timber, cedar, and the town's remaining wetlands. The second was to provide land for more consolidated farms outside the village, whether at once or in the future." On paper, at least, the Second Division represented an abandonment of the English commons system. In actuality, it took a few generations for the Second Division to be fully implemented. Even though the commons were privatized, common grazing persisted for some time. And the Great Meadow and Great Field remained as patchworks of privately owned, jointly managed strips into the 19th century.

The End of Meadow-Powered Agriculture

As Concord's population grew, more and more land was put into tillage. By the late 1700s, a point had been reached where the supply of manure could not keep pace with the needs of all the planting fields. And here the farmers hit a wall. They could not increase the size of their herds in order to produce more manure because every bit of river meadow had already been brought under the scythe. The natural meadows were at capacity.

Faced with this dilemma, Concord's husbandmen evinced a streak of Yankee ingenuity. They decided to grow "English" hay — timothy, red clover, and redtop — on the uplands. As a result of this innovation, they were able to enlarge their herds and, as a corollary, their supply of dung. The farmers fed their own livestock meadow hay, and supplemented with English hay when necessary. Surplus English hay became an important cash crop. With the larger herds made possible by the additional provender, the farmers could produce more cheese and butter to sell in regional markets.

Thus, the simple decision to grow English hay transformed Concord's largely subsistence economy into a market economy and created a new prosperity. Farmers began to find still other ways to participate in regional markets. They gave up their staple bread, a mix of rye and corn, and began purchasing wheat from the Middle Atlantic states. Farmers also began sowing oats; horses had become a popular means of late 18th century transportation. Since more fields could now be put to plow, it made sense to clear more land, and cutting woodlands yielded another readily saleable item — firewood.

This agricultural boom was purchased at the expense of the land, which became exhausted. Although the farmers enriched the tilled fields with manure, they shortchanged hay fields and pastures. Furthermore, they did not practice crop rotation. Even clover, a leguminous plant that restores nitrogen to soil, must be rotated every year or two, or the soil will become low in other important nutrients. As fields and pastures became depleted, the farmers abandoned them and cleared new land — until, by the middle of the 19th century, there was no more land to clear.

On top of that, flooding had become a serious problem in the meadows again. The farmers believed that the Billerica dam, installed in 1798 several miles north of and downstream from Concord, further aggravated the flooding problem, especially after a less permeable, higher dam replaced it in 1828. To make a bad situation worse, in the 1850s the city of Boston began the practice of releasing stored waters from "compensating reservoirs" during the late summer — at the precise time when dryness in the meadows was most crucial.

However much the farmers blamed these and other externalities, they were themselves partly responsible for meadow flooding. By the mid-1800s, the town was all but deforested. Woodlands soak up precipitation, but denuded land, especially hillsides, cannot absorb rain fast enough to prevent it from running off into lowlands, streams, and rivers. Whatever the causes, by the late 19th century, the river meadows had become virtually unusable due to flooding and prolonged wetness.

Thoreau described the hay harvest in the Great Meadow in his journal entries of August 5th and 7th, 1854, thus:

> We are now in the midst of the meadow-haying season,
> and almost every meadow or section of a meadow has
> its band of half a dozen mowers and rakers, either
> bending to their manly work with regular and graceful
> motion or resting in the shade, while the boys are
> turning the grass to the sun…

I look over the Great Meadows.* There are sixty or more men in sight on them, in squads of half a dozen far and near, revealed by their white shirts. A great part of the farmers of Concord are now in the meadows, and toward night great loads of hay are seen rolling slowly along the river's bank — on the firmer ground there — and perhaps fording the stream itself, toward the distant barn, followed by a troop of tired haymakers...

Thoreau might have been writing about the harvest in the Great Meadows two centuries earlier. The scene has a deceptive air of timelessness, changelessness. But, in reality, Thoreau was witnessing the twilight of the age of meadows in Concord.

---

* Note Thoreau's use of the plural.

PART III

African Americans in the Great Meadows

John Jack

The unornamented gray slate headstone* that marks the grave of John Jack stands at the back of the Old Hill Burying Ground, a little apart from the tidy rows of stones that stripe the ancient knoll. Inscribed on the surface is the following memorial:

> God wills us free; man wills us slaves.
> I will as God wills; God's will be done.
>
> Here lies the body of
> JOHN JACK
> A native of Africa who died
> March 1773, aged about 60 years.

---

* This gravestone is a replica. Around 1830, the Honorable Rufus Hosmer of Stow raised money from fellow members of the Middlesex Bar to replace the broken original.

Tho' born in a land of slavery,
He was born free.
Tho' he lived in a land of liberty,
He lived a slave.
Till by his honest, tho' stolen labors,
He acquired the source of slavery,
Which gave him his freedom;
Tho' not long before
Death, the grand tyrant,
Gave him his final emancipation,
And set him on a footing with kings.
Tho' a slave to vice,
He practised those virtues
Without which kings are but slaves.

John Jack was the first of several African Americans to make a home in the Great Meadows. His remarkable epitaph is clearly more than a eulogy; it is also a political statement. It was written by Daniel Bliss, the Tory lawyer who had drawn up John Jack's will and been designated by that will as his executor. Esquire Bliss is pointing to the hypocrisy of those who longed to be free of England's supposed tyranny while holding fellow human beings in bondage. He further declares that God does not condone slavery and that he, Daniel Bliss, sides with God. Adam Tolman contends, in his lecture entitled *John Jack, The Slave, and Daniel Bliss, the Tory,* that this inscription is "the first statement that [he had] been able to find anywhere, of the fundamental thesis of the later abolitionists, that slavery is in itself a sin, contrary to the will of God."

John Jack was slave to Benjamin Barron, who resided at what is now 249 Lexington Road and who made a living as both a farmer and a shoemaker. When Benjamin Barron died in 1754, John Jack was appraised as part of the estate, and his value established at £120. Slaves were legally allowed to hire out their own time when not required by their master's family, and by diligent moonlighting (possibly without the Widow Barron's knowledge), John Jack was able to buy his freedom in 1761 at the age of 48.

John Jack soon acquired six acres of plowland in the Great Fields, and later purchased a two-and-a-half acre lot on the ridge overlooking the Great Meadows, where he built a small home. He augmented his livelihood as a farmer with cobbling and handyman jobs. At his death in 1773, his estate encompassed, in addition to the eight and a half acres, a pair of oxen, a cow and calf, farming implements, a Bible and psalter, and seven barrels of cider. He bequeathed it all to Violet, another of the Barron family's slaves, but Violet may not have benefited from John Jack's largesse, since slaves were not allowed to own property. The cider testified to the only vice he was known to have; the Bible and psalter witness to the virtues Bliss ascribes to him, for John Jack was a church member in good standing.

The Robbins and Garrison Families

The next freed slaves to live in the Great Meadows were Caesar Robbins and his second wife,* Rose Bay. Caesar had received his liberty from Simon Hunt in 1780, when Massachusetts abolished slavery. He and Rose built a one-story cottage in the vicinity of John Jack's home, presumably in or near a wooded area of the ridge, because that area came to be called "Caesar's Woods."

Edward Jarvis states, in *Houses and People of Concord: 1810-1820,* that Rose and Caesar's daughter married Jack Garrison, a fugitive slave from New Jersey. Jack Garrison was certainly married, but to whom is an open question. A careful review of the *Records of Births, Marriages and Deaths (RBMD), Concord, MA:*

---

* Caesar's first wife, Catherine Boaz, died in 1806, her daughter Mary having predeceased her.

1635-1850* fails to establish a familial relationship between the Robbinses and Mrs. Garrison. Perhaps Edward Jarvis simply assumed that Jack's wife was Caesar and Rose's daughter without verifying that to be true, or perhaps Mrs. Garrison was the Robbinses' adopted child.

The Garrisons lived in a one-story cottage close by the Robbinses, conceivably the house that John Jack built. Jack Garrison worked as a self-employed woodcutter, and reportedly made a good living at his trade. According to Edward Jarvis, the Great Meadows black families:

> had good houses, well furnished and kept neatly. They had plenty to eat and to wear. Some of the ladies in the village in their walks called there and now and then were invited to tea. Mrs. Robbins and Mrs. Garrison always received them cordially and, as they were good cooks, they entertained their company in pleasant and comfortable manner. No white laborer's families were more respected.

---

* According to the *Concord Town Record of Births, Marriages, and Deaths,* a John Garrison married a Susan Middleton in 1812. Putting aside the discrepancy between the surnames, Susan could not have been the Robbinses' birth child since Rose and Caesar were married in 1807, the year after Caesar's first wife died. It is possible that Susan was an older *adopted* child who retained her surname. On the other hand, perhaps the John Garrison who married Susan Middleton was not, in fact, the *black* Jack Garrison. This argument has some merit because the RBMD does not at any time refer to *John* Garrison (or Susan Middleton, for that matter) as black but, on the two occasions it mentions *Jack* Garrison, it specifically refers to him as a black or a Negro. Moreover, the RBMD reports that Jack's three-day old child died in 1821 so, unless Jack's wife was 14 years old at the time or unless she was adopted, she could not have been the Robbinses' daughter.

Jarvis relates that the Robbins and Garrison children attended town schools, were successful students, and were accepted as equal companions and playmates by the white children.

Jack Garrison lived to become something of an institution. The February 2, 1858, *Boston Journal* article, "A Day and Night in Old Concord," described him thus:

> A living memento of the past can be seen here almost every day in the person of Jack Garrison, who is about ninety years of age. He . . . made his escape from slavery forty-five years ago, since which time he has lived in Concord. He is as active as most men at fifty, and retains his mental faculties in a remarkable degree of vigor.

Jack Garrison died in 1860 at the age of 100 years.

Peter Hutchinson

Peter Hutchinson and his family succeeded the Robbinses in their home. Henry Thoreau characterized Peter Hutchinson as "the dextrous pig-butcher." Thoreau observed that Peter often "carries home the head, taking his pay thus in kind, and these supplies do not come amiss to his outcast family." Whether the Hutchinsons were "outcast" (if indeed they were) by virtue of Peter's profession or their race is not clear.

Thoreau notwithstanding, the dextrous pig-butcher seems to have been well known and well liked in Concord. "Peter's Path" (the cart path that connected Monument Street to the Hutchinson home and to Bedford Street), "Peter's Spring" (which is located just northeast of the filter beds), and "Peter's Field" (probably sited east of the filter beds) were all, apparently, named in tribute to Peter Hutchinson. (See Gleason's map)

Jack Garrison,
fugitive slave.
(Photo courtesy of
Concord Museum,
Concord, MA. www.
concordmuseum.org)

The Peter Hutchinson
House, *which was*
moved to its present
location at 324
Bedford Road in
Concord. Formerly the
home of Caesar and
Rose Robbins.
(Photo by Maya
Gupta)

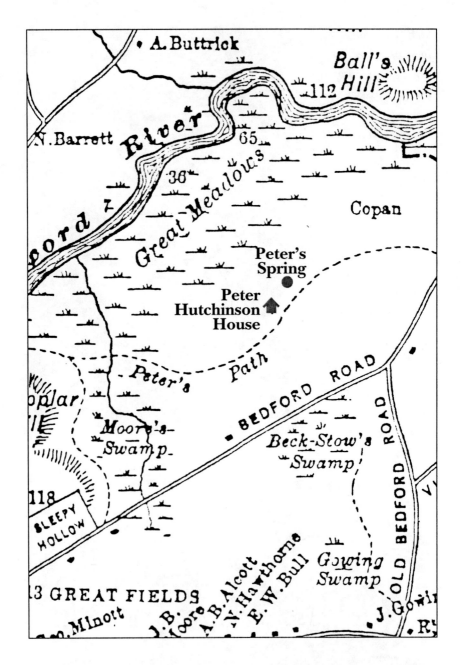

Extract from **"Map of Concord, Mass. Showing Localities mentioned by Thoreau in his Journals."** *Compiled by Herbert W. Gleason. 1906.*
Note: Peter's Spring and house added by author.

The African American residents of the Great Meadows were among a small number of ex-slaves and their children to live in Concord during the late 18th and early 19th centuries. They participated in the life of the town and were, for the most part, highly regarded by their fellow Concordians. Their influence helped catalyze the anti-slavery movement in Concord and may have prompted the town to become one of the principal stations on the Underground Railroad.

PART IV

Legendary Men of the Nineteenth Century

In the 19th century, the importance of the Great Meadows as a food source for human beings or the animals they depended upon for survival began to diminish. More and more, the Great Meadows attracted those looking for a deeper experience and understanding of the natural world. Among them were Henry David Thoreau, Concord's legendary saunterer and sage; Ralph Waldo Emerson, the leading proponent of American Transcendentalism; and William Brewster, the noted Harvard ornithologist. Like the people of prehistoric times, they left behind tokens of their experiences in the Great Meadows — in this case, their writings.

Henry David Thoreau

Henry Thoreau (1817-1862) often found his way into the Great Meadows as he ranged over the fields, woods, and waterways of his beloved Concord. Sometimes his response to the Great Meadows was a delicate lyricism: ". . . the Great Meadows, which, like a broad moccasin print, have leveled a fertile and juicy place in nature."

At other times his scientific curiosity prevailed: "I had noticed for some time, far in the middle of the Great Meadows, something dazzlingly white, which I took, of course, to be a small cake of ice on its end, but now that I have climbed the pitch pine hill and can overlook the whole meadow, I see it to be the white breast of a male sheldrake.*"

More often, Thoreau combines a poet's sensibility with a scientist's inquisitiveness, as the following excerpts from his *Notes on New England Birds* show:

> July 3, 1860
> Looked for the marsh hawk's nest (of June 16th) in
> the Great Meadows. It was in the very midst of the
> sweet-gale** (which is three feet high), occupying an
> opening only a foot or two across. We had much diffi-
> culty in finding it again, but at last nearly stumbled on
> to a young hawk. There was one as big as my fist, rest-
> ing on the bare, flat nest in the sun, with a great head,
> staring eyes, and open gaping or panting mouth, yet
> mere down, grayish-white down as yet, but I detected
> another which had crawled a foot one side amid the
> bushes for shade or safety, more than half as large
> again, with small feathers and a yet more angry, hawk-
> like look. How naturally anger sits on the young
> hawk's head!

Not content to merely *visit* the Great Meadows and notice what there was to notice, Thoreau went specifically in search of the marsh hawk's nest. Despite considerable difficulty in finding it, he persisted. In this instance, and in many others reported in his journals, Thoreau gives the impression of a conscientious

---

* Thoreau is probably referring to a common merganser; shelducks are an Old World species.

** Sweet gale is sweet flag, a waterside plant of the arum family.

landholder checking on his estate. He seems to have a personal interest in the creatures of his domain and a desire to know how they are getting on.

> March 28, 1859
> As we were paddling over the Great Meadows, I saw at a distance, high in the air above the middle of the meadow, a very compact flock of blackbirds advancing against the sun. Though there were more than a hundred, they did not appear to occupy more than six feet in breadth, but the whole flock was dashing first to the right and then to the left. When advancing straight toward me and the sun, they made but little impression on the eye, — so many fine dark points merely, seen against the sky, — but as often they wheeled to the right or left, displaying their wings flatwise and the whole length of their bodies, they were a conspicuous mass. This fluctuation . . . reminded me of those blinds whose sashes are made to move all together by a stick, now admitting nearly all the light and now entirely excluding it; so the flock of blackbirds opened and shut . . .

This metaphor — so vivid, so original — reveals Thoreau's particular genius as one of America's first nature writers.

Ralph Waldo Emerson

Philosopher, poet, and essayist Ralph Waldo Emerson (1803-1882) spent many youthful hours in the Great Meadows in the company of his brothers Edward and Charles. Their particular haunts included Peter's Field and Caesar's Wood on the ridge above the meadows, discussed in Part III. According to Edward Emerson, Ralph's son, "There they wandered and dreamed, talked of their heroes, and recited to each other or to the birch-trees the resounding verses that delighted them."

Emerson memorialized these halcyon days in the poem, *Dirge*, several verses of which are printed below. An astute reader of Emerson's poetry will know that the first and second stanzas included here can also be found in *Peter's Field*, a poem which also recalls Emerson's brothers. "Peter" refers to Peter Hutchinson, who lived on the ridge overlooking the Great Meadows, and the "lonely field" in *Dirge* belongs to Peter.

> Knows he who tills this lonely field,
> To reap its scanty corn,
> What mystic fruit his acres yield,
> At midnight and at morn?
>
> In the long sunny afternoon,
> The plain was full of ghosts;
> I wandered up, I wandered down,
> Beset by pensive hosts.
>
> The winding Concord gleamed below,
> Pouring as wide a flood
> As when my brothers, long ago
> Came with me to the wood.
>
> But they are gone, the holy ones
> Who trod with me this lovely vale;
> The strong, star-bright companions .
> Are silent, low, and pale.
>
> My good, my noble, in their prime,
> Who made this world the feast it was,
> Who learned with me the lore of time,
> Who loved this dwelling place!

> They took the valley for their toy,
> They played with it in every mood;
> A cell for prayer, a hall for joy, —
> They treated nature as they would.
>
> They colored the horizon round;
> Stars flamed or faded as they bade,
> All echoes hearkened for their sound,
> They made the woodlands glad or mad.

In these stanzas, Emerson still grieves for his lost brothers, but his grief is softened by the Great Meadows landscape, where he can so easily conjure up tender memories of them.

William Brewster

A generation after Thoreau recorded his observations of an infant marsh hawk and a flock of blackbirds, another birder plied the waters and tramped the lowlands of the Great Meadows and, like Thoreau, kept a journal of his sightings. William Brewster (1851-1919), curator of the Harvard Museum of Comparative Zoology and first president of the Massachusetts Audubon Society, "came to be regarded as our first field ornithologist," according to his friend, Daniel Chester French. Brewster's studies centered on the Great Meadows and he left 40 years of field notes on the natural history of those meadows and other Concord sites. He lived in Cambridge but spent his summers in Concord, either at October Farm on Monument Street, or at the camp he built at the base of Ball's Hill, directly across the river from the Great Meadows. (See map)

Many of Brewster's field observations in Concord are collected in two books — *October Farm* and *Concord River* — compiled by his friend, the Reverend Smith Owen Dexter (for many years rector of Trinity Church in Concord), and his colleague Thomas Barbour. These two volumes, published posthumously and therefore not edited by Brewster, attest to what Daniel Chester French called "[Brewster's] distinct literary gift."

The following excerpt from *October Farm* gives an idea of Brewster's meticulous regard for detail, as well as his finely tuned ear for birdsong. Note that he never saw any of the birds he heard that night; he identified and located them by sound alone.

> June 6, 1898
> River Birds on a Rainy Night
> . . . very near the river bank three Short-billed Marsh
> Wrens were singing, not interruptedly or at wide inter-
> vals, as most diurnal birds sing when heard at night,
> but steadily, continuously and with really exceptional
> vigor . . . . There were only three Carolina Rails
> singing on the entire stretch of the Great Meadow to-
> night but they kept it up without the slightest cessation
> as long as I was within hearing. One had a peculiar
> double note at the beginning, the call being really of
> three instead of the normal two syllables, thus: er-'er-e.
> This is the first variation in the song of this species
> that I remember of having heard [sic]. The song of
> the Carolina Rail is most nearly like the scatter-call of
> the Quail but it also suggests the peep of the Hylas.*
> Despite its plaintive, almost sad quality, it is to my ear
> one of the most pleasing sounds that one hears in our
> fresh-water meadows.

The October 11th journal entry from *Concord River* demonstrates that, once Brewster spotted a bird, he did not just tick it off his life list and move on. He continued to observe it until he lost sight (or sound) of it.

---

*A hyla is a tree frog.

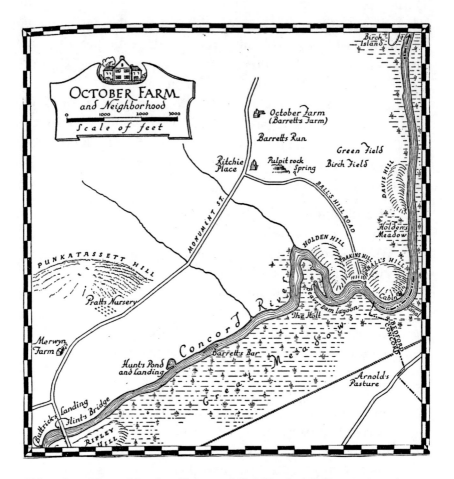

Taken from **Map of October Farm and Neighborhood** *(Frontispiece of*
Concord River: Selections from the Journals of William Brewster.
Illustrated by Frank W. Benson. By permission of Harvard University Press)

October 11, 1894
One of the most interesting experiences of my stay at
Concord this autumn happened October 29
[September 29?] with what I took to be a Short-eared
Owl. Will Stone and I had been passing the day at
Ball's Hill . . . and, as we were approaching the head

of Beaver Dam Rapids, a large bird suddenly came out of the gloom which shrouded the meadows on our left (the sun had set half an hour or more before) and after circling over the river alighted on the top of a tall pole . . . at the water's edge. Here it sat bolt upright for a minute or more, bobbing its head slowly up and down by lengthening and shortening the neck, in the manner of most Owls. Against the strong afterglow in the west it stood out most distinctly . . .

Presently it took flight again and skimmed about over the meadows, flying very gracefully but in an erratic manner very like a big moth or perhaps still more like a night-hawk, alternately appearing and disappearing as it rose against the light in the west or dipped down close to the surface of the ground. After a few minutes it returned to the stake. Its manner of alighting and taking flight was very abrupt and decided. It flew a second time soon after this and did not again return. On the evening of November 1st I saw what appeared to be the same bird, beating the meadow at the Holt* [see map] very much in the manner of a Marsh Hawk and on the next evening an Owl of similar size and appearance started from a maple opposite this meadow as I was passing.

In his 1949 book, *The Birds of Concord,* Ludlow Griscom, then research curator of Harvard's Museum of Comparative Zoology, acknowledges his debt to William Brewster: "Having now spent some thirteen years in studying Brewster's field work and records, it is my humble opinion that he was one of the greatest and most naturally gifted field ornithologists that America has ever

---

*A holt is a wood or copse.

produced." In order to help his readers understand Brewster's achievements, Griscom observes that Brewster had no "textbooks, bird guides, song manuals, records of bird-songs, prism binoculars, powerful telescopes or the use of an automobile." Griscom defends Brewster's practice of taking specimens: "The present generation must realize that looking through a glass was a waste of time in 1870 [presumably because the forerunners of the prism binoculars were of inferior acuity]; it was impossible to identify many species in many plumages without shooting them." Brewster, although a sharp critic of uncontrolled hunting and slaughter of birds for their feathers, was an expert shot, and he always looked forward to his annual hunting trip with Daniel Chester French.

The tombstone on William Brewster's grave in Mt. Auburn Cemetery is appropriately inscribed with the following verse from the second chapter of the Song of Solomon:

> Lo! The winter is past, the rains are over and gone;
> the time of the singing of birds is come.

As long as birds sing in the Great Meadows, William Brewster should be remembered and honored for his contributions to ornithology.

PART V

Sam Hoar: A Legacy of Waterbirds

A great company of Canada geese, two or three hundred strong, is stopping over in Concord's Great Meadows en route to its winter camp. The more restless of these travelers begin to advocate a return to the airway. Discussion and debate follow this proposal. Geese cluck, honk, and bark in all quarters of the ponds: "Oh, do we have to go? I like it here... I'm too tired. Can't we start tomorrow?... All right, I'm coming, I'm coming." At last, the organizers tire of consensus-building: they flap their broad wings and slowly lift off, followed by another two or more dozen geese. The group makes a grand sweep over the ponds and trumpets a final invitation. Then — they are gone. This process is repeated time and again, as muster after muster leaves the safety of the Great Meadows for the strenuous journey south. Except for the occasional drone of planes going to and from Hanscom Air Force Base, a lonely silence settles on the ponds.

The setting for this annual drama was created by Sam Hoar, who transformed the colonial haying meadows into a series of ponds that attract migratory waterfowl. In 1944, Sam and his wife Helen donated approximately 250 of their 320 Great Meadows acres to the United States Department of the Interior, Fish and Wildlife Service, "to be held in perpetuity as a Wildlife Sanctuary." The Refuge was to be located about one and a half miles

Samuel Hoar
(Photo courtesy of the Social Circle in Concord)

northeast of Concord center and bounded "Northerly by the Concord River; Easterly by the boundary between the towns of Bedford and Concord; Southerly by . . . a branch line of the Boston and Maine Railroad; Westerly by a fence running . . . in a straight line from said River to said Railroad."

The photograph accompanying Egbert Newbury, Jr.'s biography of Sam (in *Memoirs of Members of the Social Circle in Concord, Sixth Series*) reveals a conservatively dressed man near the zenith of his legal career. The resolute, rectangular face and penetrating, intelligent eyes suggest a confident man, secure in the knowledge of his abilities and of his place in the world.

Sam's self assurance was rooted in his family history. He was the scion of an illustrious Massachusetts family that included Harvard

College's third President (Leonard Hoar) and a U.S. President (John Quincy Adams). John Hoar, who fathered the Concord/Lincoln branch of the family, is remembered for being the only man in Concord who would shelter the "Praying Indians" of Nashoba during King Philip's War and for ransoming Mary Rowlandson at Redemption Rock.

Sam's great-grandfather, Samuel Hoar, known as "'Squire Hoar," was an influential 19th century lawyer, abolitionist, and United States Congressman. His popularity was such that, according to one judge, "Mr. Hoar appeared to be in every case, so that apparently the only obstacle to his having a complete monopoly of the business lay in the impossibility of being on both sides at once." His son, "Judge" Ebenezer Rockwood Hoar, became a justice with the Massachusetts Supreme Judicial Court, a United States Congressman and an Attorney General under President Grant. Judge E. R. Hoar was married to Sarah Sherman, daughter of Roger Sherman, signer of the Declaration of Independence.

Sam was born in Concord in 1887 to Samuel Hoar (son of Ebenezer Rockwood Hoar) and his wife Helen Putnam Wadleigh. In his early years, Sam seemed unlikely to achieve the stature of his distinguished ancestors. His great passion was the outdoor life. He kept pigeons, raccoons, squirrels, owls, crows, snakes, and foxes as pets. His favorite outings consisted of rowing or swimming Concord's rivers and exploring on foot or horseback the town's byways. By the time Sam enrolled in the charter class of Middlesex School in 1901, he was far more interested in studying the natural history of the woods outside the school than in mastering the school's curriculum. Sam could probably have told where the goshawk nested, where the fox kept its den, and where wild blackberries could be found, but his command of geometry and history was less informed.

Given his scant attention to academics, it is not surprising that he received, at the end of his third year, an unsatisfactory report from the headmaster, Frederick Winsor. As graduation approached, the exasperated headmaster threatened to withhold recommendations for college and permission to take the college entrance exams. Sam was sufficiently shaken that he applied himself to his books and, reportedly, achieved the best average score on the exams of any Middlesex senior. Still, this did not prevent Headmaster Winsor from writing to Harvard that

> I send him to college with some misgivings. I can best describe his character by saying that the characteristics of his family are very strong in him, – confidence in himself, fearlessness, a somewhat thick skin… Unless he is held pretty closely to the mark, I should be rather surprised if he does not become an early candidate for probation . . .

Unfortunately, Winsor's fears proved well grounded. By midterm of his first year at Harvard, Sam had been placed on probation. The stuffy lecture hall could not compete with such open-air diversions as fishing, coon hunting, and canoe tilting with friends at Staples Camp on Fairhaven Bay. Moreover, Sam had also discovered the amusements that Cambridge and Harvard offered, including debutante parties, the Hasty Pudding Club, and the football team. Despite these diversions, Sam managed to graduate from Harvard College and embark on studies at the Harvard Law School. From that point, he focused his energies on his chosen profession as a trial lawyer, and eventually excelled at it.

One of his most noteworthy victories included the International Hydro-Electric case, an early test of the liability of boards of directors, in which he won for his client the then fantastic settlement of $13 million. He also played a decisive role in forging legislation that enabled the state to control the highway billboard nuisance. But his career trophy was the investigation he led for the special legislative commission that inquired into the selling of paroles and pardons. Sam pursued that case like a ferret going after a mole. His "fearlessness" and "thick skin" stood him in good stead, and his work helped put a stop to the illicit trafficking in pardons and paroles.

Meanwhile, Sam had married Helen Van Voast Warren (whom their daughter Virginia Hoar Frecha described as "a city girl from New York") on June 6, 1914. During the first years of their marriage, they lived in the historic Grapevine Cottage, where their daughter Cynthia was born. The family then moved to #158 Main Street (now Concord Academy's Admadjaja House), which had been the home of 'Squire Samuel Hoar. It was here that the Hoar's other two children, Virginia and Sam, were born.

In 1927, the family moved into the brown clapboard Colonial Revival house designed for them by Sam's friend, Andrew Hepburn (one of the architects who helped John D. Rockefeller restore Colonial Williamsburg). This new home was built on Great Meadows Road, a cart path which at one time branched off into the haying meadows while the main trail, known formerly as Peter's Path, continued to the ridge above the meadows. When Sam and Helen moved into the house on Great Meadows Road, the old cart path was being used by "honey wagons" bringing their odiferous cargo from Concord Center to the filter beds. Sam lost no time in persuading the Town to declare Great Meadows Road a private way, thus forcing the wagons to reach the water treatment plant by way of Bedford Road.

The Great Meadows in 1927 was a place that history had passed by, of little interest to anyone but hunters and a few haymakers. Sam Hoar had a grand plan that would put the area back on the map. He would transform the counterpane of old haying fields into a staging area for migratory waterfowl. Initially, Sam probably intended this domain as a private game park for the exclusive use of his hunting friends and family. Luckily for future generations of bird watchers and nature lovers, Sam had a change of heart, and the Great Meadows will forever be open to all — except, ironically, hunters.

Piece by piece, the Hoars began acquiring the old haying lots. Many of those tracts retained their First Division forms as long, narrow strips running from the river to the ridge. As these lots came under the Hoars' ownership, Sam started to reshape the terrain. Two embryonic ponds — "duck holes," as they were called — already existed. Sam expanded the area around the duck holes and excavated the remaining marshland until he had achieved a uniform depth of about 18 inches.* He then constructed dikes out of the dredged soil and gravel he had extracted from the side of the ridge. One dike ran from the gravel pit to the river and the other, an 1,875-foot diagonal, bisected the future wildlife refuge. Great Meadows Road acted as a dike, as well. Sam probably reinforced it with mud and gravel and, if the Town had not already installed a culvert or a spillway, he undoubtedly did so. Four basins emerged from Sam's earth-moving activities. (See map) Streams, rain, and floodwater filled the basins, and these newly created ponds attracted the flora and fauna that make up a pond community.

This process must have been well underway in a very short time because, by 1929, the reconfigured Great Meadows was already attracting huge numbers of birds, many of them new to the area. Frank G. Jason, in an article entitled "Concord Marsh Developed into Great Bird Sanctuary" in the *Boston Post* of January 8, 1950, writes:

> By September of 1929 there were 2,000 ducks in the
> marsh and many of them had bred there. At the
> height of fall migration, there were sometimes several
> thousand more. But that was only part of the story.
> The marsh became known as a haven for many other

---

* The actual excavation work was carried out by Stephen Flannery of Lincoln under Sam's direction. Stephen Flannery and his workers had also excavated Sam's house site and uncovered the Indian settlement.

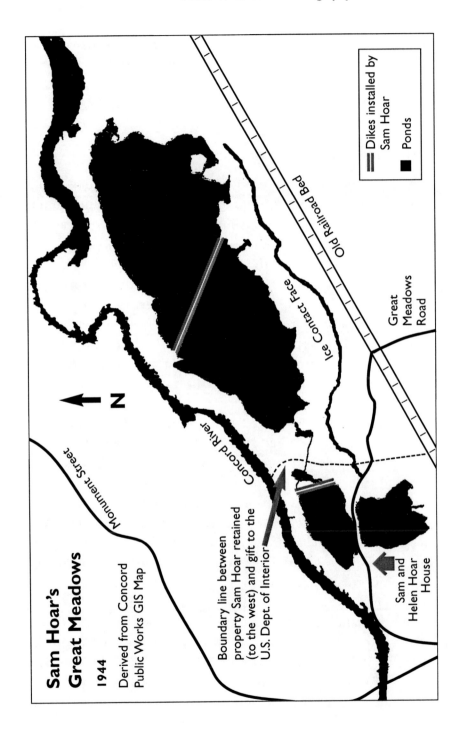

Sam Hoar's
Great Meadows

1944

Derived from Concord
Public Works GIS Map

Boundary line between
propery Sam Hoar retained
(to the west) and gift to the
U.S. Dept. of Interior

Dikes installed by
Sam Hoar

Ponds

Monument Street

Concord River

Ice Contact Face

Old Railroad Bed

Great
Meadows
Road

Sam and
Helen Hoar
House

N

kinds of wildlife species: long and short-billed marsh wrens, coot, pied-bill grebes, the common varieties of heron, the least bittern, various kinds of rail . . . and many other species of ducks hitherto unknown in recent generations.

Would that William Brewster could have been there!

As the ponds took shape, Sam began posting the edges of his property "No Trespassing," setting off a furor among the hunters who were in the habit of shooting in the Great Meadows. However, the hunters soon discovered that "they were getting better duck gunning along the edges of the refuge through the entire season than they ever had known before," according to Jason. "Overnight, instead of looking at him as a person who had deprived them of their sport, they looked at him as a person who had produced . . . a sport far beyond their greatest expectations." Even so, another furor arose when Sam, in making his gift to the Department of the Interior, retained limited hunting rights for himself and his son.

Sam eventually abandoned gunning in the Great Meadows, fearing that hunting would "burn out" the birds. Besides, Helen was afraid of guns and hated the thought of wild creatures being shot and killed. Out of deference to her, Sam sought other venues for his sport, such as the Musketaquid Club in Concord and wilderness areas in New Brunswick and North Carolina. The practice by local gunners of hunting from the Concord River and other areas on the perimeter of the Great Meadows would continue and greatly aggravate visitors and refuge managers in the years to come.

Notwithstanding the initial controversy over Sam's handling of the Great Meadows, the Hoars played a central part in the social and civic life of the town. "They were like the king and queen of Concord," according to Virginia. Helen made friends easily and actively. Sam took on many leadership positions in the community, serving as chairman of the Board of Selectmen, trustee of the Concord Free Public Library, member of the Standing Committee of First Parish, member of the Water and Sewer Commission, town moderator, trustee of Middlesex School, and a participant in numerous ad hoc town committees.

Shortly before her death in February of 2001, Virginia reminisced about her childhood in the Great Meadows. Her father wanted Virginia to have a fox for a pet, but "It was scared of me and I was scared of it, so I got a soup rabbit instead." She and her siblings adapted readily to the rhythms of life on a pond. In the winter, they would have skating parties, and her multi-acre "rinks" were the envy of her friends. When the ducklings hatched in May and June, the Hoar children would have the fun of watching the fluffy yellow babies bobble and dart in the water. In the summer months, the children canoed to the far reaches of the ponds or joined their parents on river excursions to William Brewster's

Sam Hoar and Friends Fox-Hunting *From left, Page Browne Sr., Sam Hoar, Mason Foss, Henry Vose Greenough. (Photo courtesy of A. Page Browne)*

camp, then owned by the Buttrick family, at Ball's Hill. And in the fall, the great waterfowl migrations would begin, and Sam would take his son Sammy hunting.

Toward the end of his life, Sam grew disenchanted with the town he had served so well and given so much. Concord was growing and becoming more developed; Sam was especially aggravated by the noise of planes flying into and out of Hanscom Air Force Base. He sought a quieter, more rural life. He found it in Stow, where he and Helen built their retirement refuge amidst woods, with a stream running through and a fine prospect over open fields. There Sam Hoar died on August 18,1952.

Egbert Newbury, Jr., in his memoirs of Sam Hoar, leaves unanswered the question of why Sam decided to relinquish 22 parcels of the Great Meadows to the U.S. Department of the Interior. Newbury merely comments: "It was a thoughtful, generous and valuable gift to his fellow men by one who, as Clement Ford [a lifelong friend] truly said, 'was instinctively a true son of Nature. . .'"

PART VI

Dick Borden and the Private Great Meadows

A pair of common mergansers glides low over the pond and skitters to a touchdown. The two float for a while, riding low in the water, occasionally submerging for a quick bath. These uncommon visitors to the Great Meadows make a striking couple — the male with his long, gleaming white body, black back, holly-green head, and red sawbill; the gray female with her chestnut head and ragged crest that flutters jauntily as she swims. Mergansers, unlike the more often seen dabbling ducks, are divers. As if to prove that distinction, the female suddenly disappears under the water, resurfacing several yards distant, a fish squirming in her beak.

Meanwhile, a man watches intently from his leafy baffle, carefully takes aim and shoots — film. Dick Borden, accomplished wildlife cinematographer, records every detail. His equipment includes the camera-gun (a camera mounted on a rifle stock) he designed to enable him to photograph birds in slow motion. He is working on location in Concord's Great Meadows, his home.

When Sam Hoar decided to leave Concord in 1951, he knew exactly the person he wanted to carry on his legacy: Dick Borden. According to Betsy Borden Carlson, Dick's daughter, "Mr. Hoar knew Dad would care for the ponds, dikes, surrounding woods and, most importantly, the migratory waterfowl using the ponds each year." Why did Sam Hoar repose so much confidence in Dick

Borden, who was 23 years his junior? Sam had met Dick through Sam's friend, Henry Greenough, the uncle of Dick's first wife, Betty McGinley. Sam recognized in the younger man an accomplished naturalist and a dedicated conservationist. Like Sam, Dick had developed his zeal for the out-of-doors and acquired a working knowledge of natural science as a boy. Dick grew up in Fall River, Massachusetts, on a spit of unspoiled land that jutted into Watuppa Pond — an ideal laboratory for learning about freshwater animals and their habitat.

Dick continued his study of biology at Harvard University. After his graduation, he accepted a commission from the Smithsonian Museum of Natural History that took him to the remote Peace River Region of northeastern British Columbia. There he spent

Dick Borden and His Camera Gun *(Photo courtesy of Brownie Borden)*

three and a half months studying the mountain sheep that inhabited this wilderness, exploring their territory, and taking specimens of the native mammals for the museum's collection. The Boone and Crockett Club, a century-old organization dedicated to "preserving our hunting heritage and . . . furthering conservation education," published an extract of Dick's Peace River journal in the same volume in which an essay by Theodore Roosevelt appeared.

Following the Peace River trip, Dick worked for a time in the family's textile business before joining the Navy in 1942. He received the Purple Heart and the Bronze Star for his war service. After his discharge in 1945, Dick turned to the environmental field for employment, beginning with the National Audubon Society. He later joined the National Wildlife Federation (NWF) as its first executive director, and it was at NWF that he became interested in wildlife photography. As time went by, his conviction grew that this was his true vocation and the best way for him to contribute to the conservation movement.

In early spring of 1951, Betsy made her first visit to the Great Meadows. " My dad brought my brother Spen and me to Concord for a canoe trip in the Wildlife Refuge. The water in the marshy land was high at the time, so we could canoe right over to Mr. Hoar's lower dike. Dad said, ' This is the property I most want to have.'" To Betsy, it seemed like "an impossible dream, given its grand scope compared to [the Borden family's] 18th century colonial house in Milton on a busy road." But within a few months, Dick received a call from Sam Hoar, who offered him the opportunity to buy the private Great Meadows. So, in 1952 Dick was able to launch his own film production company, Borden Productions, in the home of his dreams — a setting that offered almost inexhaustible subject matter for wildlife photography.

Over the next 30 some years, Dick would document the "wonders of the wild" in the Great Meadows, as well as in locations all over the world. The 26-part television series of the same name would eventually air on the Discovery Channel. It established Dick's reputation and opened many new opportunities for him to use his considerable skills. Dick's 1955 Disney film, *The Vanishing Prairie,* received an Academy Award as "best documentary." He contributed wild geese footage, much of it from the Great Meadows, to the Disney feature, *Those Calloways,* as well as the shorebird photography for MGM's *The Sandpiper,* the Elizabeth Taylor/Richard Burton movie. Dick again drew upon the Great Meadows for *A Canada Goose Adventure* distributed by Encyclopedia Britannica, as well as for *Tinker the Otter* distributed by Films, Inc. Tinker was Dick's pet.

After his remarriage in 1963, Dick worked in partnership with his second wife, Beatrice (Brownie) Brown. Although Brownie had brought to the marriage five school-age children, she still found the time to assist her husband with his cinematography. She also became a photographer in her own right, and some of the pictures she took during her travels with Dick formed the basis of her children's book, *Wild Animals of Africa,* published by Random House in 1982.

Despite the multiple commitments of his production company, Dick stewarded his corner of the Great Meadows as Sam Hoar might have hoped. He installed a trickle-tube system to link the upper, stream-fed pond to the lower pond, and the lower pond to the Wildlife Refuge's upper pond. (See map) He carved two small duck holes out of the western end of lower pond for the convalescence of injured birds. Dick assiduously maintained the dikes, filling in the holes and tunnels made by muskrats. More than once he was mistaken for the hired man, as he chugged along on his red backhoe, attired in a pair of baggy khakis and an old Navy shirt.

In an effort to attract a diversity of wildlife to his property, Dick initiated a gadwall-seeding project in his ponds with the Delta Waterfowl Research Station in Delta, Manitoba. Gadwalls are a gray marsh duck not known to have bred in the Great Meadows. Over an eight-year period, Dick released in the Great Meadows

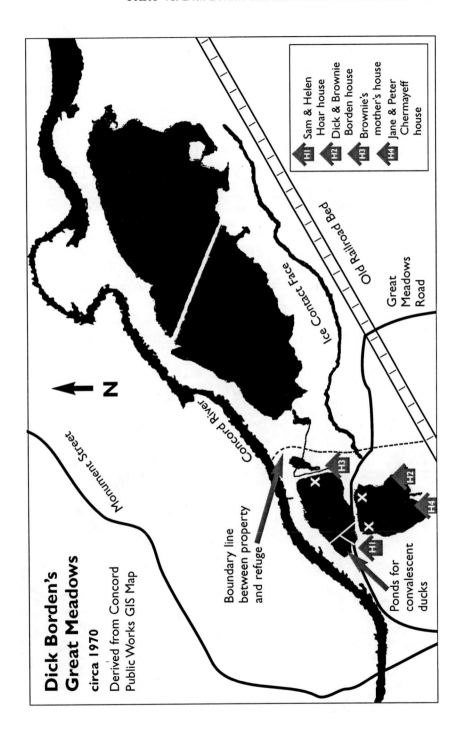

Dick Borden's Great Meadows

circa 1970

Derived from Concord Public Works GIS Map

N

Monument Street

Concord River

Boundary line between property and refuge

Ponds for convalescent ducks

Ice Contact Face

Old Railroad Bed

Great Meadows Road

H1 Sam & Helen Hoar house
H2 Dick & Brownie Borden house
H3 Brownie's mother's house
H4 Jane & Peter Chermayeff house

more than 75 juvenile gadwalls, hatched by captive parents in Manitoba, in the hope they would become breeding residents. Subsequently, eight wild broods were known to have hatched in the Borden ponds. Two or three breeding pairs moved to the Great Meadows National Wildlife Refuge, and about a dozen appeared within a five-mile radius of the Borden ponds. Dick and his partners at Delta hoped that their study would inspire other owners of private reserves to undertake gadwall seeding. (Unfortunately, no gadwalls are known to have reproduced in the Great Meadows since 1990.)

Dick welcomed visitors to his ponds, sometimes offering to teach a child the rudiments of fishing. Not once did he post his property during the 35 years of his tenancy. So strongly did Dick

Brownie and Dick Borden *(from the Borden family archives)*

Borden become identified with his Great Meadows property that locals still refer to the ponds in the private Great Meadows as "the Borden ponds."

Throughout the time he lived in the Great Meadows, Dick continued his involvement in the conservation movement, serving as president of the Massachusetts Audubon Society, trustee of the North American Wildlife Foundation, chairman of the conservation committee of the Boone and Crocket Club, and member of the Massachusetts Governor's Council on Open Space and Outdoor Recreation. The Trustees of Reservation bestowed on Dick their annual Conservation Award in 1973.

Dick and Brownie eventually sold the house that Sam Hoar built to Dick's cousin, the late Ames Stevens. They moved to a ground-hugging, shingled house of their own design near the head of the upper pond. A few years later, Brownie's mother, Mary Allen Brown, built a house above the old gravel pit overlooking the lower pond. In 1970, Dick's daughter Jane and her husband Peter Chermayeff, founder of the architectural firm Cambridge Seven Associates, built their international style home on a peninsula at the head of the upper pond.

By the age of 76, Dick had grown tired of meeting deadlines for his production company, and he no longer had the stamina to maintain his Great Meadows property. He and Brownie decided to retire to Santa Barbara, California, where Dick took up a new interest — sculpture — with an enthusiasm that came close to his passion for photography. Dick died in 1999 at the age of 89. Betsy describes the family gathering in the Great Meadows to scatter Dick's ashes over the lower pond: "As we were saying our last farewells to Dad, a large flock of Canada geese wheeled in and settled on the water. Dad's spirit — full of love and nature and wildlife — filled us all."

PART VII

The Trials and Triumphs of the Refuge Manager

Ed Moses (1967-1969)*

A sandy-haired man wearing the U.S. Fish and Wildlife Service's regulation taupe cap and khaki uniform steps out of his Dodge pickup and heads down the dike trail. Ed Moses walks briskly to the mid-point of the dike, where he stops for a moment to enjoy the commanding view of the entire sanctuary. He surveys the great shimmering pools that reach from ridge to river and the manifold forms of bird life that float on, stand in, hover over, and soar above the water. As he continues along the dike, he gradually shifts his focus from the panoramic to the close-up: green darners chasing midges in the trefoil, a row of painted turtles basking on a log, and a partially submerged bullfrog peeping out of the muddy waters.

By the time Ed has completed his circuit of the impoundments, he has formed an opinion on how the wetlands are functioning and what steps he should take to improve their health. This is Ed's first appointment as a refuge manager (he was an assistant refuge manager in his previous job), but he harbors no reservations

---

* Dates inside parentheses refer to term in office.

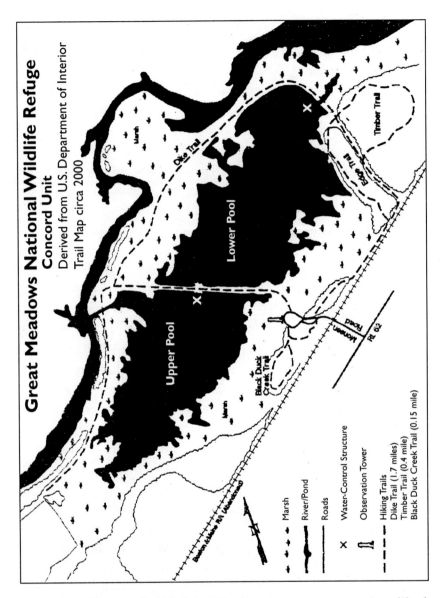

about his ability to do this job. His experiences constructing diked wetlands at the Iroquois National Wildlife Refuge in New York and at the Erie National Wildlife Refuge in Pennsylvania have prepared him for this position, and he is eager to put his stamp on the Great Meadows National Wildlife Refuge (GMNWR).

Ed became the Great Meadows' first resident manager in 1966, 22 years after Sam and Helen Hoar made their generous gift to the U.S. Department of the Interior. The parcel had been considered too small to warrant an on-site manager, so it was administered as a satellite of the Parker River National Wildlife Refuge. However, in the 1960s, the Massachusetts Division of Fisheries and Wildlife (MDF&W), at the urging of Sudbury Valley Trustees' Director Alan Morgan, targeted a 12-mile strip of wetlands along the Sudbury and Concord Rivers for preservation. This strip was at high risk for development. Protected wildlife corridors alongside rivers are crucial because they extend the territorial range for both aquatic and terrestrial animals and allow populations to interbreed. Luckily, the federal Fish and Wildlife Service (USFWS) already owned a critical piece of that corridor — the former Hoar property — and had the funds to purchase additional land. By 1966, USFWS had acquired approximately 2,500 acres (including the Hoar land), and the agency badly needed a refuge manager to signpost the new property and enforce the regulations that govern public use. Enter Ed Moses.

Although Ed was, technically, an "on-site" manager, in fact his base of operations was in the attic of the historic Old Manse in Bedford and his "site" included a rather far-flung empire that reached from Framingham in the south to Billerica in the north. Shortly after his arrival, Ed rented more central quarters near the railroad tracks in Concord Center — a closer location, to be sure, but hardly "on-site."

When Ed began posting the new GMNWR parcels, he encountered members of the public hunting, cutting wood, or engaging in other activities that were now prohibited. In order to persuade people to discontinue these activities, Ed used a non-adversarial approach he called "educational law enforcement." He would courteously explain that the land had become part of the National Wildlife Refuge and usage was now restricted to such activities as hiking and nature study. Ed's goal was to win support, not just acquiescence. Although, according to Ed, this approach resulted in a 98% compliance rate, a few offenders "failed the attitude test" and repeated their violation — at which time Ed would issue a citation.

After Ed had finished posting the new GMNWR property and had made a good start in educating the public on appropriate use of the protected land, he was able to turn his attention to management of the Concord unit's wetlands. The refuge manager's primary tools for regulating such an environment are well-constructed dikes and linking mechanisms that allow water to move through the ponds (called "impoundments" or "pools" by refuge staff). Water flow is essential to the health of a wetland because it allows the water to mix with air and capture oxygen. Dissolved oxygen is a precondition for much aquatic plant and animal life.

Prior to Ed's arrival, Parker River staff had installed an overflow spillway in the main dike to connect the lower and upper pools, and another spillway to serve as the lower pool's outlet to the Concord River. This rudimentary system helped evacuate water from the impoundments after the spring floods that had so bedeviled colonial farmers. A more fundamental benefit of the spillways was that they facilitated water flowage from the upper impoundment, which was (and is) fed by Dick Borden's lower pool, to the refuge's lower impoundment and out to the river.

Ed augmented this system by having local contractor John Bordman, who later built the observation tower for the refuge, install a water control structure not far from each spillway. These structures consisted of a half-circle riser (vertical intake pipe); a cement pad to anchor the riser; and two 20' heavy-gauge, corrugated metal pipes running horizontally under the dike. The risers could accommodate stoplogs — pieces of wood that could be moved to regulate the water level in the impoundments. Ed's water control structures were similar to the trickle tubes that Dick Borden placed in the private Great Meadows. By removing stoplogs from the lower pool's control structure, Ed could backflow water from the river into that impoundment when it dried out in the late summer or early autumn. He could also draw down water from either pool to encourage the growth of food-bearing native plants to feed the fall avian migration.

Of course, the dikes had to be kept in good repair for the system to function properly. Sam Hoar had constructed the dikes out of mud dredged from the marshes, and marsh mud tends to sink as the organic materials within it decompose. In March of 1968, a particularly heavy flood caused water levels to rise by six feet. Floodwaters eroded the dikes and dislodged floating mats of cattail, some an acre in area and four to seven feet thick, and deposited them on the dikes. Several days of bulldozer action and a thousand tons of gravel were required to put things right. Dike maintenance would prove to be a never-ending headache, not to mention a budget-breaker, for Ed and his successors.

Although the water-control infrastructure gave Ed a degree of *mechanical* control over the flow of water, he had little or no control over the *chemical* make-up of the water. The water treatment plant on the ridge above the refuge was pumping nitrogen-rich, chlorinated water into the upper pool. Chorine is a toxic chemical and potentially harmful to all animal life. Ed was alarmed to find numerous dead frogs in the outfall pool. Frogs are a good indicator of how other wetland species, such as fish and turtles, are being affected, and Ed was especially worried about possible effects on the threatened Blandings turtles.

The nitrogen and other nutrients in the effluent created an algal bloom on the ponds. "The eutrophication [decay] level was terrific — there was barely enough dissolved oxygen to sustain fish life." The decaying algae exuded an overpowering stench. Algae is the foundation of the pond food chain and, as such, it is "as important to a pond. . . as grass is to a field of grazing cows," according to Michael J. Caduto writing in *Pond and Brook*. But clearly this was an instance of too much of a good thing. Ed and his USFWS colleagues wanted the Town of Concord to extend the treatment plant's pipeline into the Concord River where, in theory at least, the moving waters would dilute the impact of excess nutrients. Town officials were reluctant to allocate the funds for such a pipeline. More than a decade would pass before the matter was resolved, and then only after Bill Ashe, Deputy Regional Director, threatened legal action against the Town by the U.S. Fish and Wildlife Service.

Purple loosestrife — that strikingly beautiful invader — had already taken up residence in the Great Meadows by the time Ed got there. An alien like purple loosestrife can spread through an ecosystem almost unimpeded because the system has not developed biological controls to contain it. As a result, the invading species crowds out native plants that offer animals more nutritional value and more useful habitat. Ed annually documented the steady spread of the loosestrife up and down the GMNWR by aerial photography. He also initiated a research project with 54 study plots to determine whether the loosestrife could be curtailed by mechanical means — either hand-pulling or hand-cutting. Unfortunately, the 1968 flood destroyed the study plots, and purple loosestrife seemed to flourish and expand in the wake of the flood.

Before Ed began his term as Great Meadows' refuge manager, staff from the Parker River NWR had discovered that the number of wood ducklings hatched each summer had been declining. Consequently, Massachusetts Division of Fisheries and Wildlife biologist Dave Grice had begun a wood duck nesting study in the refuge, and when Ed came to the Great Meadows, he supported the research effort.

Dave and his assistants would begin monitoring nesting boxes at the end of March. As each clutch of eggs neared the end of its incubation period, the researchers would test the eggs by trying to float them in the pond. If an egg floated, the duckling was about to hatch. From then on, the researchers would visit the nest daily until they discovered a pipping egg. They would then shut the hen inside the box by stuffing the opening with burlap. The following day, the researchers would find the ducklings hatched and dry inside the box. Dave Grice's team would band the wood hen and, as the babies followed her out of the box, they would attach a numbered web tag to each one. Tagging enabled the researchers to track the ducklings from each brood over time.

The survival of wood ducklings was jeopardized by the overpopulation of snapping turtles, for whom baby ducks are a readily available seasonal treat. Ed brought in John Rogers, a turtle harvester who claimed that he caught snappers using his own unique method of "calling" them. In 1967, John removed 193 snappers, the largest weighing more than 60 pounds. He sold the turtles to New York City restaurants.

Ed transferred to the Parker River National Wildlife Refuge in April 1969. The problems with which he grappled — pollution from the water treatment plant, the invasion of exotic plant species, the decline of wood duck production, and the erratic behavior of New England's weather — would continue to dog his successors.

Arthur (Lee) Tibbs (1969-1970)

Lee Tibbs occupied the refuge manager's seat for only one year, during which he continued the initiatives begun by Ed Moses. A sandhill crane visited the sanctuary during Lee's term, an event as remarkable then as it is in our own time. Lee reported this sighting to the Massachusetts Audubon Society. The Audubon was "dubious," since sandhill cranes are rarely seen in Massachusetts, but "all doubts were dispelled when Dick Borden . . . verified the sighting." As this incident suggests, the refuge managers maintained an ongoing collegial relationship with Dick Borden during the years Dick lived in the Great Meadows.

The low point of Lee's term was a misadventure with an explosive that had an untoward effect on the windows and televisions in neighboring houses. Lee had contracted with the U.S. Army Demolitions Unit from Fort Devens to blast out the cattail mats that obstructed the lower pool's water control structure. They undertook this project in winter, when the impoundments were frozen, so the shock waves were transmitted through the air. If the procedure had been attempted in the summer, the water and underlying mud would have absorbed the impact of the blast.

Lee left the Great Meadows to pursue doctoral studies at Colorado State University in 1970.

Larry Malone (1970-1973)

When Larry Malone took over in the summer of 1970, he noticed that "the impoundments still lack[ed] the emergent vegetation they had prior to the 1968 flood." In response, he introduced drawdowns of the upper pool during the summer months, resulting in the growth of smartweed, chufa, and water millet. He reported that water birds fed heavily on these grains when the pond was refilled in the fall. As Larry demonstrated, drawdowns are an effective management tool for stimulating desirable vegetation. Experience in other freshwater impoundments suggests that drawdowns attract herons and related birds and help control invasives.

Dave Grice's wood duck study continued, and the results continued to be disappointing. In 1970, wood duck production dropped to the unprecedented low of 48 young hatched, compared to 268 in the baseline year of 1963. The explanation for this decline eluded refuge staff. A study conducted by Neil Johnson of the University of Massachusetts demonstrated that lower protein diets adversely affected wood duckling growth and survival. But were Great Meadows wood ducks protein-deprived? Or were they, for some reason, reluctant to use the nesting boxes? Assistant Refuge Manager Berlin Heck undertook a study to determine whether the use of artificial eggs in unoccupied nests encouraged hens to use those nests. The results were negative.

Larry noted in his annual narrative of 1971 that the "duckweed mats" (the term used by several refuge managers to refer to floating mats that contained both algae and duckweed) now covered three quarters of the pools. Although marsh and shore birds feed on duckweed and the insects it attracts, algae in this quantity was suffocating the ponds. On the other hand, American lotus had also become established in the refuge, and Larry reported that the lotus provided good cover for wood ducks and teals, and that wood ducks fed on lotus seeds. A later refuge manager would take a dimmer view of the American lotus.

Public use of the Great Meadows National Wildlife Refuge had more than doubled since Ed Moses' time — 46,602 visitors in 1972 as compared to 20,201 in 1968. Although many of those visitors went to GMNWR property in Sudbury, Bedford, and other towns, most came to the Concord impoundments, drawn by the variety of waterfowl. Larry sighted, during his three-year term, glossy ibises, least and American bitterns, American [great] egrets, six species of gulls, a mute swan, common gallinules, North and Wilson's phalaropes, white-rumped and western sandpipers, and Caspian terns — in addition to the more typical Great Meadows birds. The educational programs offered by Larry and his staff — bird walks, refuge tours, wildlife demonstrations — also promoted visitor use.

Grady (Gene) Hocutt (1973-1974)

Larry Malone moved on in 1973 and Gene Hocutt served as refuge manager from October of that year through April 1974, too short a span to have a measurable impact. Still, he made one decision that would have history-making consequences: he hired Linda Gintoli as assistant refuge manager. When Gene left, Linda became the first female refuge manager in the entire U.S. Fish and Wildlife system.

Linda Gintoli (1974-1977)

Linda believed that "the refuge ha[d] the potential of becoming a major Environmental Education center of the nation," and she put her energies into realization of that potential. She developed an environmental curriculum for the public schools and, using an old log cabin as her base, began training teachers in the use of that curriculum. She hosted a meet-the-neighbors kind of public meeting, "Great Meadows Update," as a means of enlisting the support of area residents, began writing a column on environmental issues for a local newspaper, and appeared on a radio program called *Future Earth.*

Linda continued the drawdowns introduced by Larry Malone and was gratified by the fine crop of littoral (shore-side) native plants that resulted. However, the drawdowns had two unanticipated consequences. The first was that "*unfortunately* [sic], the lowered water has allowed American lotus to get a strong foothold." Linda decided to eliminate the lotus through the application of Aquathol Plus.* Linda's action is puzzling. In addition to the food and cover value mentioned above, this native water lily provides a microhabitat for insects and snails, and a resting place for frogs and dragonflies. The herbicide proved ineffective over two consecutive summers. However, the Japanese millet Linda

---

*Aquathol is a dipotassium salt of endothall. A Virginia Cooperative Extension pamphlet, *Pesticides and Aquatic Animals: A Guide to Reducing Impacts on Aquatic Systems,* ascribes high toxicity to endothall. However, the EPA's Consumer Factsheet on Endothall states that the herbicide is "not likely to accumulate in aquatic life."

planted in 1977 produced an excellent crop, and the millet proved to be "an efficient means of curtailing the American lotus."

The second unexpected effect of the drawdowns was an outbreak of botulism in which 60-100 ducks died. Avian botulism is a deadly disease that causes progressive paralysis in its bird victims. Water level fluctuations and poor water quality are two of the conditions associated with avian botulism. In this case, the timing of the drawdown — July and August — triggered the outbreak. According to Ed Moses, "May and early June are the latest that you should initiate dewatering of an impoundment." Mid- to late-summer temperatures "superheat shallow water and the dark mud beneath, creating a medium ideal for the growth of botulin." The poor quality of Great Meadows water no doubt also contributed to the botulism occurrence. The wastewater treatment plant was, by 1977, emitting *one million gallons of effluent per day* into the Great Meadows. Linda re-opened conversations with the Town of Concord and the Environmental Protection Agency to address the issue. Meantime, drawdowns were discontinued.

Human beings were both a bane and a blessing during Linda's tenure: "Drinking parties and vandalism reached outrageous proportions during the summer months" of 1976, and she and her assistant, Tom Mountain, had to share late night patrols with the Concord police. On the other hand, severe funding cutbacks forced Linda to turn to the Youth Conservation Corps (YCC) for volunteer help. YCC youth riprapped the dikes, built a boat launch, and performed other essential maintenance jobs.

Dave Grice concluded his 15-year study of wood duck production in 1977, and his findings (see chart) suggested that wood ducks might be on the rebound. The years 1970 to 1973 were clearly the low points, but the data from 1974 through 1977 show an increase in hatchlings. However, the total number of hatchlings in 1977 was still half of what it had been in the bumper crop

Table 1: Results of 15-year Wood Duck Production Study
Massachusetts Fish and Wildlife Service

Year	Hatchlings Upper Marsh	Hatchlings Lower Marsh	Hatchlings Total
1977	40	136	176
1976	65	41	106
1975	63	102	165
1974	38	101	139
1973	0	21	21
1972	28	30	58
1971	25	34	59
1970	20	24	44
1969	130	9	139
1968	140	48	188
1967	153	106	259
1966	128	201	329
1965	174	216	390
1964	186	188	374
1963	154	114	268

year of 1965. Dave Grice suggested that the ice storm of 1968, which destroyed half the nesting boxes, and the algae mat of 1973 accounted for the off years. Other explanations seem equally plausible: that the data simply document the natural fluctuation of a bird population over an extended period of time, or that contaminants in the river and the impoundments were having a deleterious effect on wood duck production. A later refuge manager would have yet another theory.

Linda resigned in late 1977 to accept a position in the Kenai National Moose Range in Alaska.

David Beall (1978-1984)

David Beall, Linda's successor, began the following January. His first two months of work were accompanied by three major winter storms, the third of which on February 6th brought 24" of snow and hurricane force winds. David's six-year stint in the Great Meadows would prove to be eventful in other ways, as well.

Water chestnuts made their unwelcome appearance in the refuge the year of David's arrival. Following Ed Moses' example of trying a chemical-free approach to invasives control, David deployed the YCC to hand-pull the chestnuts. But the industrious YCC workers, who pulled several *tons* of water chestnuts from the upper pond in a single summer, were no match for the chestnut. In just three years, the chestnuts took over the entire lower pool and made a significant inroad into the upper pool. David then established test plots to compare three methods of control: 1) hand-pulling; 2) cutting just below water level; and 3) covering with heavy black plastic.

David did not report on the study's results, but we know from his successor's reports that none of these interventions proved effective in containing the invasive. Refuge managers have since learned that the water chestnut seed remains viable for three to five years, so cutting the chestnuts or covering them with plastic would have no impact.

In 1979 — a banner year for the Concord impoundments — the Town of Concord finally installed a pipeline from the sewage treatment plant to the river. By this time, the duckweed/algae mat had grown so thick and wide that it might have been possible to walk on it. While environmentalists may regard the shift of a million tons of effluent per day out of the Great Meadows and into the Concord River as a dubious triumph, floating mats of algae have not since appeared in either the refuge or on the river. Duckweed, in normal quantities, is still present in the sanctuary.

Another notable event during David Beall's term was the relocation of refuge headquarters to Weir Hill in Sudbury. The GMNWR purchased the former home of the Elbanobscot Foundation, an environmental center, and began renovating it in 1981 with funds from the Bicentennial Land Heritage Program. The move to Weir Hill opened up needed space for staff offices, classrooms, and educational exhibits, giving teaching and outreach programs a boost. Despite the advantages of this move, the Sudbury location had a drawback: it concentrated programs and staff away from the Concord unit, which was by far the most frequently visited.

In 1982, approximately 96,000 people visited Concord's Great Meadows. David mentions that among them was "a gentleman scantily clad in women's purple undergarments" — a marked departure from the jeans and fleece worn by the more typical visitor. In the early years of the GMNWR, growth in the number of people using the refuge might have been regarded as a token of success. Now, it was a cause for concern.

When pondering the decline in wood duck hatchlings, David bemoaned, "It is easier to increase public use than to increase wildlife use. At the refuge, people have been winning over wildlife." David seemed to imply that the overall decrease in wood ducklings was caused by the increase in human activity, and he had some basis for that conclusion. Wood ducks are among the shiest of marsh birds; even the smallest indication of human presence causes them to take to the air with a *whoo-eek, whoo-eek,* their alarm call. Still, David's comments disregard the evidence of Dave Grice's study that wood ducks were beginning to make a comeback. (See page 73)

Whether right or wrong about a causal relationship between public use and wood duck decline, David had pinpointed a critical issue. People were the newest "invasives." Snowmobilers damaged the dikes and muskrat lodges; picnickers left trash, some of it potentially harmful to animals; and birders, bikers, and joggers occasionally disrupted nesting along the dikes. In 1978, vandals caused $6,000 worth of damage to refuge property. The question of how to achieve a balance between human use and wildlife use in a heavily trafficked sanctuary such as the Great Meadows continues to tax refuge managers.

Despite, or maybe because of, his reservations about public use, David took a proactive approach to environmental education and community involvement. Like Linda Gintoli, he invited the public to a planning meeting. The event drew 100 community participants, and input from the meeting was used to develop a public use plan. David also hired a public use planner and two outdoor recreation specialists to further develop the environmental education program. Although enactment of Proposition $2\frac{1}{2}$ dampened public school participation, scout participation increased and refuge staff reached out to other constituencies, such as the learning impaired children from the Fernald School.

David's term in the Great Meadows had begun with three blizzards. His last year, 1983, was also meteorologically exceptional. It was the wettest year (54" of precipitation) in 25 years and the warmest year in 30.

Lloyd Culp (1984-1987)

Lloyd Culp, formerly assistant refuge manager at the Okefenokee National Wildlife Refuge in Georgia, succeeded David Beall in 1984. Lloyd, like David, complained of inappropriate use of the sanctuary: "Never-ending vandalism and theft plague the Concord unit." However, he acknowledged that the GMNWR was an oasis of wild in the ever developing western suburbs, and that, as the population of the region grew, so would the pressure on such natural places. So Lloyd made it his mission to educate the public on *appropriate* use of the refuge, a task he acknowledged was "easier said than done."

It was not long before Lloyd had an opportunity to practice appropriate-use education. Hunters sitting in their boats on the river would fire at ducks and geese flying out of the impoundments — despite a Town of Concord ordinance that prohibited hunting within 500 feet of the refuge boundary. In 1985, Lloyd totally banned hunting from the river adjacent to Concord's Great Meadows, relying on a 1985 Regional Solicitor's* opinion. The essence of that opinion was that the refuge owns the bottom of the river (where it flows through the GMNWR) and can, therefore, control activities on the surface of the river or in the air above it. Lloyd and his staff made a concerted effort to reach out to Concord gunners. They held a two-day informational meeting on hunting regulations and policies; Lloyd visited local hunt clubs; and other USFWS agents made contact with hunters in the field — all in an attempt to convey that Appropriate Use, in this case, meant No Use.

Lloyd reopened the battle against water chestnuts by applying nearly 7,000 pounds of Aquakleen** in 1986. At the end of the summer, it appeared that the weed killer had vanquished the chestnuts. It also had the unintended effect of eradicating the American lotus from the upper pool. More weed killer was applied to the chestnuts the following year, but, "by the end of August, water chestnuts covered most of the pools, almost as if they had not been treated with herbicides."

At the same time as the Aquakleen was being applied to the water chestnuts, refuge staff treated the purple loosestrife with the

---

* The Regional Solicitor is a Department of Interior attorney who supervises an office of lawyers that provides legal advice to all Interior agencies in a given region. The Regional Solicitor signs all legal opinions for his/her region.

** Aquakleen is a 2,4-D derivative. According to the EPA *Consumer Factsheet on:2,4-D,* "There is no evidence that bioconcentration of 2,4-D occurs through the food chain."

herbicide Rodeo.* Lloyd noted that "more extensive applications may be required if summer drawdowns result in the expansion of the purple loosestrife infestation." It would seem that Lloyd's reintroduction of drawdowns to encourage the growth of desirable plants had the effect of also encouraging an undesirable plant — purple loosestrife.

Lloyd reported that cattails, a native plant that grows on the edge of ponds, were becoming a problem because they formed dense floating mats that blocked water flow between the ponds (as they had during Lee Tibbs' watch). Before Lloyd was forced to take corrective action, he received unexpected help from the 50-year frequency flood of April 1987, which swept the cattails from the spillways and water control structures. Troublesome as cattails can be to refuge management, they are an essential resource for the muskrat, which eats the tuber and uses the leaves and stem in den building. However, the muskrats were themselves becoming a nuisance because they tunneled through the dikes, adding to the maintenance load.

Lloyd experienced several assaults on the refuge from external sources. In addition to the destructive tides of the 50-year flood, the Great Meadows felt the fury of Hurricane Gloria's 76 miles per hour winds in 1985. Moreover, in 1986, several state agencies issued health advisories warning against eating fish from the Sudbury River, which of course feeds the Great Meadows by way of the Concord River. The Sudbury had been contaminated by mercury from the Nyanza Company that had once operated in Ashland and was now listed as a Superfund site.

---

* Rodeo is the commercial name of glyphosate, a herbicide which is rated "slightly toxic" to aquatic life by the Virginia Cooperative Extension's pamphlet, *Pesticides and Aquatic Animals: A Guide to Reducing Impacts on Aquatic Systems*. The EPA's *Consumer Factsheet on Glyphosate*, however, states that the herbicide "does not tend to accumulate in aquatic life."

Ed Moses (1988-1997)

After Lloyd Culp's transfer to the Great Dismal Swamp National Wildlife Refuge in Virginia, management of Concord's Great Meadows came full circle. Ed Moses returned in 1988 for a nine-year stint, making his 12 years of service to the Great Meadows the longest of any refuge manager.

When he returned to the Concord impoundments, Ed saw that purple loosestrife and cattail had completely taken over in the littoral zone on the upper pool. Water chestnuts covered all remaining open water. Since herbicides had proven so ineffective in previous years, Ed realized he needed a fresh approach to invasives control. He introduced thousands of beetles — Galerucella pusilla and Galerucella calmariensis — into the refuge. These natural predators of loosestrife had been tested by the United States Department of Agriculture and the USFWS. Although the beetles did not eliminate the loosestrife, they did succeed in holding it in check.

Ed also considered new options for curbing the water chestnuts. At about this time, he and Dan Monahan, Concord's Natural Resources Administrator, happened to notice the novel behavior of a muskrat. This particular rodent sat on its feeding platform, a cluster of water chestnuts before it, methodically gnawing through each hard shell to get to the viable nutlet inside. Much to Ed's regret, he never saw another muskrat eat water chestnuts, but he couldn't help thinking that a colony of chestnut-eating muskrats would have been the ideal means of biological control. He ultimately selected the aquatic weed harvester as the best alternative because it obviated the need for annual drawdowns and herbicides. When his efforts to rent a harvester failed, he initiated a successful three-year, $125,000 fund-raising campaign to purchase an aquatic weed reaper, which was delivered near the end of his Great Meadows tour.

The photograph shows Ed at the helm of the bright orange reaper, sweeping up water chestnuts from one of the ponds in the

Ed Moses *(left)* **demonstrates operation of aquatic weed harvester** *to Tim Jones of the Concord Public Works Department and Adam Ryde of the Lincoln Conservation Department. From* The Concord Journal. *June 28, 2001. (Photo by Ann Ringwood)*

Great Meadows. He was so eager to demonstrate the value of the reaper in controlling invasives that he came out of retirement to operate the harvester on its maiden run. He got a little carried away that first day, not only piloting the harvester but, at times, unloading it as well — a procedure that required him to run up and down a moving conveyer belt. On one of his descents, he slipped and broke an ankle. But such was Ed's enthusiasm for the new equipment that he had his ankle set and was back on the job the next day, and every workday thereafter for the next three months.

Muskrats, whose numbers had increased significantly — 80 lodges in 1989 versus 50 the previous year — were raising havoc with the dikes. Because of their mischief, Ed and his staff were forced to devote many extra hours to dike maintenance. Ed considered trapping the muskrats to control the population, an action the visiting public would surely have decried. In the end, he took no action, perhaps because the muskrats helped contain the cattails.

Despite Lloyd Culp's earlier efforts to educate gunners, illegal hunting continued and visitors to the sanctuary were sometimes pelted with shot. Ed decided that the only way to get compliance was to enforce the ban on hunting *for the entire length of the refuge* — in all eight towns and along all 12 miles — and not just in Concord, as Lloyd had done. Partial enforcement, in Ed's view, only confused hunters and undermined cooperation. Ed's action could have resulted in a "huge flap, but again the old educational law enforcement concept was successfully employed."

Other human encroachments on the refuge included jet skiing and motor boating on the river, both of which disturbed feeding and nesting waterfowl. Like Sam Hoar, Ed found the noise of Hanscom Field air traffic to be objectionable, although he had to admit that the refuge's wildlife adapted surprisingly well to the annoyance. When anti-Hanscom activists came to him seeking information that would support their position, he responded: "I wish I could help you, but the only organism that is adversely affected is the public."

One of Ed's experiments during his second term was the introduction of a roving docent program in which volunteers would greet visitors on summer weekends and provide them with information about the Great Meadows wildlife community. This innovation scored high marks with both docents and visitors. Ed hoped that one day a permanent visitor center would be built at the Concord impoundments, but in lieu of that, the roving volunteer filled the need for informal, on-site environmental education.

When Ed looks back at his work in the Great Meadows, he considers his most important legacy to be "finishing up the [Great Meadows] land acquisition program" begun by the USFWS in the 1960s. In his first term, he helped secure 1,150 acres for this vital wetland corridor. During his second term, he developed a partnership with Sudbury Valley Trustees and enlisted the help of then-Congressman Chet Atkins of Concord to achieve the final goal of almost 3,500 acres in eight communities under the umbrella of the

Ed Moses reaches a career milestone with the presentation of his 30-year service pin by Assistant Regional Director Don Young. (Photo courtesy of Great Meadows National Wildlife Refuge)

Great Meadows National Wildlife Refuge. Ed was instrumental in the acquisition of nearly half of this land, valued at $6.65 million in 1995. The GMNWR has continued to grow and, as mentioned earlier, now encompasses more than 3800 acres.

Ed Moses retired in 1997 after 34 years of service to the United States Fish and Wildlife Service. He and his wife Marilyn live in Danville, New Hampshire, in the barn they converted into a comfortable woodsy retreat, surrounded by trees and adjacent wetlands. Ed is busy with a new career as a woodcutter: the pick-up truck sitting in his driveway is emblazoned with the words "Have sawmill, will travel."

~

No one would say, after reading this account, that the job of the Great Meadows refuge manager is an easy one. Formidable obstacles hinder the manager in creating a balanced freshwater habitat: destructive natural phenomena, such as high winds and floods; environmental contaminants, like sewage treatment effluent; acts of misuse by members of the public, unauthorized hunting and vandalism among them; the invasion of exotic species, including water chestnuts and purple loosestrife; and, often most daunting of all, inadequate information about what interventions work. Who would want this job?

But the work of the refuge manager is not without its rewards, even triumphs. The millet and wild rice the refuge manager planted in the spring becomes a Thanksgiving feast for thousands of migratory waterfowl six months later. The Town finally installs an outflow pipe from the sewage treatment plant to the river, and the ponds begin to cleanse themselves of chlorine and excess nitrogen. When money becomes scarce, volunteers come to the rescue — riprapping the dikes, pulling water chestnuts, serving as tour guides and teachers. After prolonged negotiations, a family decides to donate a significant chunk of land to Fish and Wildlife, adding yet another vital piece to the Great Meadows corridor. The manager guides a group of children through the refuge. They are enchanted by the frogs, birds, turtles, and dragonflies, and full of questions about it all. Who *wouldn't* want to be a refuge manager?

Conclusion

People have been coming to Concord's Great Meadows for 13,000 years. Each successive group has sought something different: foodstuffs, fodder for livestock, a place to call home, a natural world to study or savor, recreation, replenishment for the spirit. The human history of the Great Meadows is not just the story of why people came to this place, but also of what they left behind. Prehistoric peoples left behind a great many tools for hunting and for processing food. Colonial farmers no doubt left drainage ditches and fences, though Sam Hoar's excavations would have expunged those remnants of the haymaking years. In compensation, Sam Hoar left his ponds and dikes.

Peter Hutchinson's house and John Jack's tombstone are reminders of the African American era in the Great Meadows. Others who are part of the Great Meadows story left a legacy of a different order: Thoreau and Brewster's journals, Emerson's poetry, Dick Borden's films. And the diked wetlands of the National Wildlife Refuge are a contemporaneous testament to the refuge managers and their staff who have worked (and continue to work) to maintain a thriving freshwater community in our midst.

Today, human beings are encroaching upon Concord's Great Meadows as never before. The Great Meadows National Wildlife Refuge estimates that in the 12-month period ending October 31, 2003, more than 514,000 people visited the refuge or participated in its programs. A GMNWR spokesperson estimated that approximately 60-70 percent of the total — 300,000 to 360,000 — visited the Concord unit in that period. While the majority of visitors come and go without harming the sanctuary, a few misuse or abuse the refuge, as we have seen in the previous section. The greater damage, however, is frequently perpetrated by people — acting individually or in organizations — who may never have even set foot in the sanctuary.

Norman Boucher, in an article entitled "No Refuge" in the *Boston Globe Magazine* of August 15, 1993, characterizes the Great Meadows National Wildlife Refuge as "a small patch of poisoned wilderness." Among the poisons that have been found in the Sudbury and Concord Rivers are mercury, lead, arsenic, and chromium – all in quantities well in excess of an established standard for "highly polluted sediments." Polychlorinated byphenyls, or PCBs, have also been detected, and in amounts that could adversely affect reproduction in birds that ingest contaminated fish. These toxins can be traced to companies that have operated or are operating riverside.

The Next Chapter in the Great Meadows Story

What can you do to help reclaim and protect Concord's Great Meadows? As a visitor, follow the precept, *Leave No Trace.* Carry out your litter. Resist the temptation to pluck a cattail or other plant. Take pains not to disturb the animals or inadvertently harm them. Bikes, barking or off-leash dogs, intrusive birders, and groups of runners can disrupt shoreline nesting.

Even outside the refuge, your actions can have an impact. Avoid growing potentially invasive species in your garden; wind or birds may carry the seeds to the Great Meadows or a nearby wetland. If you live in the watershed of the Assabet, Sudbury, or Concord Rivers, or near a stream that might feed the Great Meadows, make sure you do not allow pollutants into the water. Support organizations like Sudbury Valley Trustees and

Organization for the Assabet River in their efforts to clean up the river system and prevent further contamination.

If you have reached this point in the Great Meadows story, you are probably interested enough in the sanctuary to participate in some of the Wildlife Refuge's educational programs or to offer your skills as a volunteer. For further information, you can reach the Great Meadows National Wildlife Refuge at (978) 443-4661.

Part VIII of *Concord's Great Meadows: A Human History* will be written about us, those of us whose lives are somehow connected to the Great Meadows, whether public or private. What will be *our* legacy? What will *we* leave behind?

Sources

Part I: The Old Ones and What They Left Behind

Blancke, Shirley. "Musketaquid: The Native Experience." *From Musketaquid to Concord*. Concord, MA: Concord Antiquarian Museum. 1985.

Braun, David P. and Braun, Esther K. *The First Peoples of the Northeast*. Lincoln, MA: Moccasin Hill Press. 1994,

Dee, Charles. Interview with author. April 20, 2001.

Dincauze, Dena Ferran. "The Northeast." *Common Ground: Archaeology and Ethnography in the Public Interest*. Washington, D.C.: National Park Service. Spring/Summer 2000.

Dincauze, Dena Ferran. "Introduction." *From Musketaquid to Concord*. Blancke, Shirley and Robinson, Barbara. Concord, MA: Concord Antiquarian Museum. 1985.

Loring, Stephen. "Prehistoric Concord," four-part series. Concord, MA: *Concord Patriot*. July 12, 19, 26, August 2, 1979.

Robinson, Barbara. "From Musketaquid to Concord: Trading Places." *From Musketaquid to Concord*. Concord, MA: Concord Antiquarian Museum. 1985.

Smith, Benjamin L. Unpublished notebooks. Concord, MA: Concord Antiquarian Museum. 1932. (Courtesy of Shirley Blancke)

Part II: The New Pioneers

Concord Town Records. Volume 2, page 39.

Donahue, Brian. "The Forests and Fields of Concord: An Ecological History." *The Social History of a New England Town, 1750-1850*. Waltham: Brandeis University. Fall 1983.

Donahue, Brian. "Henry David Thoreau and the Environment of Concord." *Thoreau's World and Ours*. Eds. Edmund A. Schofield and Robert C. Baron. Golden, CO: North American Press. 1993.

Donahue, Brian. *The Great Meadow: Farmers and the Land in Colonial Concord, Massachusetts*. New Haven, CT: Yale University Press. 2004 (forthcoming)

MacLean, John C. *A Rich Harvest*. Lincoln, MA: Lincoln Historical Society. 1988.

Scudder, Townsend. *Concord: American Town*. Boston, MA: Little, Brown and Company. 1947.

Shattuck, Lemuel. *History of the Town of Concord*. Boston, MA: Russell, Odiorne, and Company. Concord, MA: John Stacy. 1835.

Walcott, Charles H. *Concord in the Colonial Period*. Boston, MA: Estes and Lauriat. 1984.

Part III: African Americans in the Great Meadows

"A Day and a Night in Old Concord." *Boston Journal*. Boston, MA. February 2, 1858.

Concord Town Records. *Births, Marriages, and Deaths*. Concord, MA 1635-1850.

Elliott, Barbara K. and Jones, Janet W. *Concord: Its Black History, 1636-1860*. Concord, MA: Concord Public Schools. 1976.

Fenn, Mary R. *Old Houses of Concord*. Concord, MA: Old Concord Chapter, Daughters of the American Revolution. 1974.

Gross, Robert A. *The Minutemen and their World*. New York, NY: Hill and Wang.1976.

Jarvis, Edward. *Houses and People in Concord, 1810 to 1820*. Unpublished typescript from 1882 manuscript, annotated and with references by Adam Tolman. Concord, MA: Concord Free Public Library. 1915.

Tolman, Adam. "John Jack, the Slave, and Daniel Bliss, the Tory." Lecture delivered before Concord Antiquarian Society, Concord, MA. March 4, 1889. Published by Concord Antiquarian Society as Pamphlet No.6, 1902.

Trumbull, Joan. *Concord and the Negro*. Unpublished manuscript. Poughkeepsie, NY: Vassar College. 1944.

Wheeler, Ruth R. *Climate for Freedom*. Concord, MA: The Concord Antiquarian Society. 1967.

Part IV: Legendary Men of the Nineteenth Century

Blanding, Tom. "Readings and Remarks for Musketaquid Earth Day, at the Great Meadows, Concord." Unpublished speech. Concord, MA. May 3, 1997

Brewster, William. *Concord River.* Cambridge, MA: Harvard University Press. 1937.

Brewster, William. *October Farm:* Cambridge, MA: Harvard University Press. 1936.

Emerson, Edward. "Ralph Waldo Emerson." *Memoirs of Members of the Social Circle in Concord, Second Series.* Cambridge, MA: The Riverside Press. 1888.

Emerson, Ralph Waldo. *Poems.* Cambridge, MA: The Riverside Press. 1904.

Gordon, Jayne. "Thoreau and Friends: Curriculum Development Project" funded by EDCO/Seefurth Foundation. Concord, MA 1999.

Griscom, Ludlow. *The Birds of Concord.* Cambridge, MA: Harvard University Press. 1949.

Rusk, Ralph L. *The Life of Ralph Waldo Emerson.* New York, NY: Charles Scribner's Sons. 1949.

Thoreau, Henry David. *A Week on the Concord and Merrimack Rivers.* Orleans, MA: Parnassus Imprints, Inc. 1987.

Thoreau, Henry David. *Notes on New England Birds.* Ed. Francis H. Allen with assistance from William Brewster and Dr. Charles W. Townsend. Cambridge, MA: Riverside Press. 1910.

Torrey, Bradford, and Allen, Francis H., eds. *The Journal of Henry David Thoreau,* Volume 6. Salt Lake City, UT: Peregrine Smith Books. 1984.

Torrey, Bradford, and Allen, Francis H., eds. *The Journal of Henry David Thoreau,* Volume 12. Salt Lake City, UT: Peregrine Smith Books. 1984.

Torrey, Bradford, and Allen, Francis H., eds. *The Journal of Henry David Thoreau,* Volume 13. Salt Lake City, UT: Peregrine Smith Books. 1984.

Part V: Sam Hoar: A Legacy of Waterbirds

Browne, A. Page Jr. Interview with author. May 9, 2001

Browne, Pierce. Interview with author. April 11, 2001

Concord, Massachusetts Historical Commission. *Survey of Historical and Architectural Resources: Concord, Massachusetts. Five volumes.* Concord, MA: The Commission. 1994.

Frecha, Virginia Hoar. Interview with author. February 8, 2001.

Hoar, Samuel and Hoar, Helen Warren. Deed transferring approximately 250 acres to U.S. Department of the Interior. Cambridge, MA: Middlesex South District Deeds, Book 6826, page 226. May 3, 1944.

Jason, Frank G. "Concord Marsh Developed into Great Bird Sanctuary," *Boston Post.* Boston, MA. January 8, 1950.

Newbury Jr., Egbert S. "Samuel Hoar." *Memoirs of Members of the Social Circle in Concord, Sixth Series.* Clinton, MA: Clinton Press Inc. 1975.

Shaw, Gordon. "Great Meadows 50th: Retrospective." Unpublished text of comments delivered at the 50th anniversary celebration of the Hoar's gift to the Department of the Interior. Concord, MA. July 11,1994.

Wilson, Leslie Perrin. *Hoar Family Papers, 1738-1958.* Unpublished manuscript. Concord, MA: Concord Free Public Library. 2001.

Part VI: Dick Borden and the Private Great Meadows

Borden, Betsy. Telephone interview with author, November 13, 2000. Correspondence and documents.

Borden, Brownie. Telephone interview with author, November 16, 2000. Correspondence and documents.

Borden, Richard. "Trip into Peace River Region 1931." *Spirit of the Wilderness.* Boone and Crockett Club. Missoula, MT. 1997.

Borden, Richard, and Hochbaum, H. Albert. "Gadwall Seeding in New England." Paper presented at the Thirty-First North American Wildlife and Natural Resources Conference, March 14, 15 and 16, 1966. Washington D.C.: Wildlife Management Institute. 1966.

Part VII: The Trials and Triumphs of the Refuge Manager

Beall, David. Annual narratives: 1978-1984. Sudbury, MA: Great Meadows National Wildlife Refuge.

Caduto, Michael J. *Pond and Brook: A Guide to Nature Study in Freshwater Environments.* Englewood Cliffs, NJ: Prentice-Hall, Inc. 1985.

Consumer Factsheet on 2,4-D. [Online] Available http://www.epa.gov/OGWDW/dwh/c-soc/24-d.html

Consumer Factsheet on Endothall. [Online] Available http://www.epa.gov/OGWDW/dwh/c-soc/glyphosa.html

Consumer Factsheet on Glyphosate [Online] Available http://www.epa.gov/OGWDW/dwh/c-soc/glyphosa.html

Culp, Lloyd. Annual narratives: 1984-1987. Sudbury, MA: Great Meadows National Wildlife Refuge.

Gintoli, Linda. Annual narratives: 1974-1977. Sudbury, MA: Great Meadows National Wildlife Refuge.

Grice, David. "Results of a 15-Year Wood Duck Production Study." Massachusetts Fish and Wildlife Service. 1977.

Locke, Louis N. and Friend, Milton. *Avian Botulism: Geographic Expansion of a Historic Disease.* U.S. Fish and Wildlife Leaflet 13.2.4. Madison, WI. 1989.

Malone, Larry. Annual narratives: 1970-73. Sudbury, MA: Great Meadows National Wildlife Refuge.

Moses, Ed. Annual narratives: 1967-69; 1988-92. Sudbury, MA: Great Meadows National Wildlife Refuge.

Moses, Ed. Interview with author. November 29, 2001.

Sears, Harry. 2003. Interview with author. February 19, 2003.

Tibbs, Arthur. Annual narrative: 1969-1970. Sudbury, MA: Great Meadows National Wildlife Refuge.

Conclusion

Boucher, Norman. "No Refuge," *Boston Globe Magazine.* Boston, MA: Globe Newspaper Company. August 15, 1993.

Index

ISBN 1412023351

9 781412 023351